THE COUNCIL ON FOREIGN RELATIONS

A Short History

GEORGE GAVRILIS

The Council on Foreign Relations (CFR) is an independent, nonpartisan membership organization, think tank, and publisher dedicated to being a resource for its members, government officials, business executives, journalists, educators and students, civic and religious leaders, and other interested citizens in order to help them better understand the world and the foreign policy choices facing the United States and other countries. Founded in 1921, CFR carries out its mission by maintaining a diverse membership, with special programs to promote interest and develop expertise in the next generation of foreign policy leaders; convening meetings at its headquarters in New York and in Washington, DC, and other cities where senior government officials, members of Congress, global leaders, and prominent thinkers come together with Council members to discuss and debate major international issues; supporting a Studies Program that fosters independent research, enabling CFR scholars to produce articles, reports, and books and hold roundtables that analyze foreign policy issues and make concrete policy recommendations; publishing *Foreign Affairs*, the preeminent journal on international affairs and U.S. foreign policy; sponsoring Independent Task Forces that produce reports with both findings and policy prescriptions on the most important foreign policy topics; and providing up-to-date information and analysis about world events and American foreign policy on its website, CFR.org.

The Council on Foreign Relations takes no institutional positions on policy issues and has no affiliation with the U.S. government. All views expressed in its publications and on its website are the sole responsibility of the author or authors.

For further information about CFR, please write to the Council on Foreign Relations, 58 East 68th Street, New York, NY 10065, or call the Communications office at 212.434.9888. Visit our website, CFR.org.

CONTENTS

FOREWORD

Following World War I, an intense debate about America's role in the world gripped the nation. Isolationists and unilateralists in the Senate defied President Woodrow Wilson and voted down the League of Nations, leaving one of the era's most powerful countries outside an organization tasked with maintaining international peace. Other Americans remained firm in their view that the United States should not retreat behind its two oceans and could only be safe if it embraced a leadership position in the world. In no small part, this lack of consensus about America's role motivated a small group of business and civic leaders to establish in 1921 the Council on Foreign Relations (CFR), endowing the organization with a mission "to afford a continuous conference on international questions affecting the United States."

The founders of CFR succeeded in creating an important American institution. But they failed to persuade their fellow citizens that their country's security was best served by an active role in global affairs. To the contrary, over the succeeding two decades, isolationism and protectionism emerged as the prevailing ideologies. It took World War II and then the Cold War to convince Americans of the need for significant, sustained U.S. international involvement.

This understanding was never complete, however. The consensus favored American involvement in the world (as opposed to isolationism), but in no way did it settle the question of the nature or extent of that involvement, as the intense and prolonged debate over the war in Vietnam made clear. Yet the basics of the country's role were widely shared. They included a defense capability sufficient to deter aggression that, if need be, could be used in a wide range of contingencies across the world; support for alliances in Europe and Asia; an embrace of free trade; and active U.S. participation in the plethora of international institutions created, in large part, by American diplomats after World War II.

The end of the Cold War, though, left the United States without a compass to guide its way in the world. Containment, the doctrine developed by the American diplomat George F. Kennan (and first made public in the pages of *Foreign Affairs*), could survive every challenge but its success. Forty years of successful pushback coupled with its own internal flaws and the person and policies of President Mikhail Gorbachev led to the dissolution of the Soviet empire and state. In the aftermath of the Cold War, which ended in a manner and on terms few optimists could even have imagined, there has been little agreement on either the ends or means of American foreign policy.

Over the past three decades, fueled in part by costly (and, to many, misguided) intervention in Iraq and occupation of Afghanistan, the debate has expanded to the most basic questions: Should the United States continue to support the country's alliances, be involved in multilateral institutions, embrace (however conditioned) free trade, and promote human rights and democracy? There is little agreement, and widely held assumptions are increasingly rare, despite the reality that many Americans along with others around the world have been on the whole well served over the past three-quarters of a century by international developments that would not have materialized absent sustained U.S. effort and leadership.

This debate will likely intensify as a result of recent crises: the epic human toll of the COVID-19 pandemic, the resulting deep economic dislocation and heightened inequality, protests over racism and police behavior, and the emergence of even deeper domestic political divisions, underscored and exacerbated alike by the horrific events surrounding January 6, 2021. Many will conclude that the United States lacks the resources, unity, and bandwidth to focus on the world when there is so much to tackle at home.

What makes the domestic debate all the more consequential is that it does not take place in a vacuum but is occurring in a world of great flux: the reemergence (or, in some cases, persistence) of major power rivalry, between the United States and both Russia and China, between China and both India and Japan, and between Russia and Europe. Meanwhile, the Middle East shows few signs of stabilizing. More than one out of every one hundred persons in the world—over eighty million men, women, and children—are either internally displaced or refugees.

What is new and different about this era, though, is the emergence of an array of challenges linked to globalization. 9/11 demonstrated the global reach of a new generation of terrorists. The COVID-19 pandemic is another example; what began in Wuhan did not stay there. Nuclear proliferation (along with the increase in the number and quality of delivery systems) continues in North Korea, while Iran has resumed activities limited by the 2015 nuclear pact. Climate change is associated with fires, violent storms, and flooding. The internet is a source of vulnerability as much as it is a lifeline.

In addition, the future role of the dollar is in some doubt, owing to massive U.S. deficits, frequent U.S. resort to unilateral financial sanctions, the emergence of cryptocurrencies, and a loss of confidence in American competence. Global trade faces new challenges as the pandemic has revealed that most countries import many critical goods from abroad, prompting new calls for a degree of domestic self-sufficiency. The pandemic has likewise strengthened calls to decouple the American and Chinese economies—above all in the technology sphere.

Alas, it is far from clear that concern over a future pandemic will lead to a material strengthening of global machinery to fight and contend with infectious diseases. Indeed, what is marked about this moment is the large and increasing gap between global challenges and threats and the willingness and ability of countries to come together to meet them. One often hears the phrase "international community," but the cold truth is that little such community exists.

What we are seeing is more like what existed when the Council was founded in the wake of World War I than any moment since. I am not suggesting that the two eras separated by a century are identical, but there are echoes: increasing isolationist, unilateralist, and protectionist tendencies in the United States; rising nationalism and populism here and around the world; the emergence of new technologies that, depending on how they are used, can enhance life or endanger it; and the inability of existing international institutions to cope. Conflict within countries is all too common; equally worrying are signs that conflict between countries is potentially more probable than many judged only recently.

The Council too exhibits similarities with the organization created a century ago. It remains committed to producing smart, serious, policy-relevant analysis for those in and out of government participating in the ongoing debate over this country's proper relationship with the world.

At the same time, the institution has taken on additional roles. One is to make international developments and foreign policy choices understandable to a much broader cross section of Americans and others, be they students and their teachers, congregational and religious leaders, state and local officials, or average citizens. The technology for doing so has necessarily expanded to include multiple websites, blogs, podcasts, and social media outlets.

The Council has also become an important engine of talent development. Over the years, literally thousands of young men and women have received their start in the field through some program, internship, or fellowship administered by CFR.

Not surprisingly, the Council itself has changed along the way. It now includes more than five thousand increasingly diverse individual members, another 150 corporate members, nearly four hundred staff, two buildings, and two websites. I expect that those who founded it would be surprised by what it has grown to become—but also, for the most part, pleased, especially as what has not changed is the commitment to the principles and traditions of nonpartisanship and independence.

This path was not inevitable; little of it was smooth or without resistance, disagreement, or controversy. In *The Council on Foreign Relations: A Short History*, George Gavrilis chronicles the Council's first century, beginning with its founding in the wake of pandemic and world war and bringing it up to the current virtual reality necessitated by the COVID-19 pandemic. Drawing on a wide range of oral histories, interviews, and documents, he describes many of the critical events, debates, decisions, and personalities that made the Council what it is today. Like any legacy institution, there are times CFR got the balance between the need to preserve and the need to change right, and other times when it failed. Gavrilis has written honestly and authoritatively about both. The result is an informative and often engrossing volume, with much to say about a venerable but dynamic institution as well as the changing country and the world it has both reflected and sought to shape.

Richard N. Haass
President
Council on Foreign Relations
January 2021

PROLOGUE

May 12, 1992—Mikhail Gorbachev leaned over the small glass case and studied the magazine, the very first issue of *Foreign Affairs*, now seventy years old and faded. Its pages were open to an article with passages underlined and pencil marks in the margins.

Foreign Affairs Editor William G. Hyland, serving as the nominal escort during Gorbachev's visit to the Council on Foreign Relations (CFR), pointed at the magazine. "You see this? This underlining was done by Lenin."

Amused and surprised, Gorbachev turned to Hyland. "Lenin? Vladimir Lenin?"

"Yeah," Hyland replied. "The editor sent Lenin an early copy of *Foreign Affairs* because there was this article about the Soviet Union."

"Really? How did you get it to him?"

"Through Karl Radek," explained Hyland.

"Oh."

"Then Radek sent it back with this underlining, so we kept it as a special exhibit."

"Do you know what happened to Radek?" Gorbachev asked.

"Yeah, you guys shot him," replied Hyland. Radek had been a rising Soviet star, an advisor to Lenin and editor of *Izvestia*—until he fell out of favor in Joseph Stalin's time.

"So, you see what happens," Gorbachev said as a photographer aimed a camera to commemorate his visit.

Gorbachev's presence was notable because he had given a Council delegation to Moscow the hardest of times back in 1987, a story that this book saves for later. And his visit, even with all the attention and accolades, must have been humbling or at least bittersweet: the

Foreign Affairs *Editor William G. Hyland with former Soviet Premier Mikhail Gorbachev*

Council had outlasted the Soviet Union, and Gorbachev was visiting as the former leader of a country that no longer existed.

• • •

These pages tell the story of the Council on Foreign Relations—the events that made its founding a reality in 1921, the people who shaped it over the decades, the global leaders and experts who spoke under its roof, the challenges that nearly derailed it, and its value to policymakers and audiences eager for a stronger footing in foreign affairs untainted by a partisan agenda.

"Part One: From War to Peace to War, 1918–68" begins in the wake of the Great War, which destroyed Europe and brought down empires. America was rising, but its political elite and public were divided on what to do with its power. As the country debated what direction to take, a core of concerned businessmen, policymakers, and academics from the Northeast were eager to pursue a multilateral, internationalist approach rather than one of isolationism and hoped to foster an informed debate on America's role in the world. Edward M. House, President Woodrow Wilson's advisor and one of the Council's founding members, wrote in *Foreign Affairs* in 1923:

> Our people, native and foreign born, cherish the belief that this Republic was created to become an instrument for the betterment of man, and not merely a pleasant and safe abiding place. They will not be content until the United States has again assumed the leadership and responsibilities in world affairs commensurate with her moral, economic, and political position.

Soon after founding the Council on July 29, 1921, a small group of members and officers launched the first programs—study groups, meetings, and dinner discussions with secretaries of state, foreign diplomats, business titans, and Ivy League professors. The Council's flagship journal, *Foreign Affairs*, started publishing in 1922, the year the Soviet Union came into being. Nearly two decades later, in a decisive juncture during World War II, Council members and officers helped a short-staffed State Department grapple with a range of wartime issues, and the Council consolidated its role as the premier international affairs institution in the United States, shaping debates and launching careers in foreign policy.

The Council fostered animated debates during the early Cold War years, but the disagreements were mostly about details of how, not whether, America should lead abroad. Over time a consensus emerged on the necessity of encouraging American internationalism, investing massive sums into rebuilding Europe, forging alliances through the North Atlantic Treaty Organization (NATO), adopting containment as an overarching strategy to deal with the Soviet Union, and fighting in the Korean War. The Council itself was an elite, northeastern institution, exclusively male in its membership and leadership. Getting a spot on the membership roster or a place at a study group table was a sign that one had arrived.

"Part Two: A Council and a Country Divided, 1969–92" examines a sustained period of crisis of purpose. The Vietnam War fractured American society and triggered bitterly divisive debates about foreign policy. It dramatically eroded the broad consensus in foreign policy, and the Council was not equipped for the challenge; much of its leadership was hawkish on Vietnam, and dissident voices did not find its environment congenial. Moreover, the Council had remained a northeastern elite institution at a time when the establishment was being questioned in the most public ways.

Many changes followed: the admission of women as members, attempts to bring in younger voices and members from minority communities, episodic successes in fundraising, and occasional meetings or publications that resonated with policymakers. But the Council was losing its competitive edge, as a growing number of think tanks, some narrowly specialized and others with partisan leanings, were taking over its audiences and the attention of policymakers. It was a massive challenge for CFR leadership, and there were times when the Council seemed to be on the verge of irrelevance. New rival journals were even outshining *Foreign Affairs*. Change would come after the end of the Cold War.

"Part Three: A New Council Emerges, 1993–2021" tells the story of two presidencies that restored the Council and its economic fortunes and refined its mission. Globalization was picking up speed, and American foreign policymakers had not yet found principles to cope with the challenges of terrorism, civil and ethnic conflict, and nuclear proliferation. Leslie H. Gelb shook up the Council in sometimes brash ways. But he brought in younger members with broader professional, geographic, and racial and ethnic backgrounds, and he expanded the Council's range of work to reaffirm its commitment to nonpartisanship, including through Independent Task Forces. He worked closely with wealthy Board members who loved the Council and gave generously.

Richard N. Haass has improved the Council's classic aspects, revitalizing the David Rockefeller Studies Program and broadening the range of meetings, and he opened the Council's new building in Washington, DC, to expand programs in the nation's capital. During his tenure, the Council has become a staff-led organization and one whose membership and leadership have become more reflective of the diversity of American society. He has expanded the Council's mission with a revamped Outreach and a new Education Program to gain audiences beyond the policymakers and experts who have historically shaped foreign policy debates while giving the public a better window into the Council's work. The changes reflected a new reality as the Council celebrated its one-hundredth anniversary in the midst of the coronavirus pandemic—that foreign policy eventually touches everything and everyone and that the public deserves to have an informed stake in the debates about America's role in the world.

PART ONE

FROM WAR TO PEACE TO WAR

1918–68

ORIGINS—THE INQUIRY

November 1918—The Great War was drawing to a close. Tens of millions had died, many in battle and even more at the hands of a raging influenza pandemic. Europe's economies were shattered, the era of empire was coming to an end, and the Bolsheviks were winning Russia's Civil War. In the United States, President Woodrow Wilson seized the opportunity to sketch his vision for a new world that included principles of collective security, national self-determination at the expense of Europe's continental empires, and a League of Nations to underwrite it all. But Wilson needed an agreement that would end the war and outline the terms of the peace, a group of well-informed international experts to give it shape, and the American public and Congress to put their weight behind his vision. He managed only two out of the three.

Shortly after hostilities ceased in November 1918, Wilson set sail with a large entourage of advisors and officials to attend the Paris Peace Conference, the formal meeting of the victorious Allies—the United States, Britain, France, Italy, and Japan—to set the peace terms for the defeated Central Powers, which included Germany, the Austro-Hungarian Empire, and the Ottoman Empire.

While State Department staff took the cushy upper decks, twenty-three scholars were relegated to the lower berths. The scholars were members of "the Inquiry," a group of over one hundred men and a few women that Wilson's aide on national security, nicknamed "Colonel" Edward M. House, had launched.

The need for this group was acute; the State Department lacked scholars and experts to prepare material that would be needed at the peace conference—memos and reports with reliable information about the political, economic, and social conditions in war-ravaged

Europe, especially the status of the territories of the losing side. Lindsay Rogers, a distinguished professor at the University of Virginia and subsequently a Council member, recalled that he was asked to prepare a memorandum for the Inquiry on international control of Macedonia, a large, multiethnic European province that the Ottoman Empire had lost. He declined, as his interests at the time were in American constitutional law and British politics. It was only from the invitation that he learned that Macedonia was subject to international control.

Rogers saw it as a worrying sign that the Inquiry sought help from people who were not always knowledgeable on the subjects at hand, writing in a 1964 issue of the *Geographical Review*:

> Washington as an international capital had been hardly more important than Brussels, and Belgium, because of her international position and her colonial empire, had more "experts" than the United States. Area specialists in America were very few . . . so students of history and government were called on to deal with matters that were foreign to them.

The Inquiry did what it could to make up for the dearth of expertise, recruiting accomplished scholars and professionals who would later be part of the Council as members or directors. These included James T. Shotwell, a Columbia University historian; Isaiah Bowman, a renowned geographer; David Hunter Miller, a New York lawyer who distinguished himself in Paris as a draftsman and made up for his somewhat nepotistic appointment (he was a partner with House's son-in-law); and Walter Lippmann, a young and controversial author who had risen fast to become a founding editor of the *New Republic*.

As the negotiations in Paris wore on in the early months of 1919, members of the Inquiry shared their frustrations with one another. Some felt sidelined by Wilson and territorial State Department officials, others were embarrassed that European diplomats saw the American president as unsophisticated, and almost everyone was disappointed with the proceedings, which were awash in disagreement over how much Germany and its allies should be punished and made to pay for the war. At one point, an unwell Wilson left the conference for several days, leading participants to speculate whether he had been stricken with influenza—the pandemic compounded the toll of the war, killing 675,000 Americans that year and tens of millions in other countries. The American public was eager to put the war behind

Members of the Inquiry aboard the USS George Washington *en route to the Paris Peace Conference, 1918*

it, and, as the Council's first anniversary book publication expressed it, "under the pressure of a public opinion which was impatient to be done with war-making and peace-making, decisions had to be taken in haste."

On the margins of the contentious proceedings, the Americans who made up the Inquiry and a few diplomats they had befriended along with their like-minded British counterparts committed to stay in touch. In May 1919, just before the Treaty of Versailles was signed, the British and Americans met at the Hotel Majestic in Paris and proposed forming an Anglo-American Institute of International Affairs to sustain their work and suggest policies to guide the postwar order.

The British contingent went home and got to work putting together an institute, while, according to Peter Grose in *Continuing the Inquiry: The Council on Foreign Relations From 1921 to 1996*, the Americans returned to encounter "isolationism and prohibition, thoroughly inhospitable to the ideals of the League of Nations." Their mood soured further when the U.S. Senate rejected both the Treaty

of Versailles and the League of Nations. Dejected and scattered across a number of East Coast cities, the group lost its drive, and the idea to form an Anglo-American Institute of International Affairs went dormant for nearly a year.

Then three things happened that revived the group. First, the British contingent launched the Royal Institute of International Affairs—informally known as Chatham House—to great fanfare, and the news traveled fast. Second, an enterprising woman from New York learned that an American branch had been discussed but had not materialized. She created an organization using the name "the American Institute of International Affairs" and managed to secure financial support. She printed stationery and letterhead and invited people to join, including some who had been part of the initial idea in Paris.

Following pages: The Hall of Mirrors, Versailles, during the signing of the peace treaty, June 28, 1919

Former Secretary of State Elihu Root was named honorary president of the Council.

Fearing the loss of their claim to the institute, several members of the original group jumped to action, "whereupon a few words were had with her sponsor and the financial support was withdrawn," according to the Council's first anniversary book.

Third, a little-known club called the Council on Foreign Relations that had formed at the war's end decided to disband in early 1921, possibly dispirited by the election victory of Warren G. Harding, an opponent of the Treaty of Versailles and Wilson's multilateralism. The club's energy fizzled along with its finances, but it drew on an impressive list of members, all of them New Yorkers working in high-level banking, finance, legal, and manufacturing positions and all concerned that any turn away from internationalism would hurt postwar business. They were interested in resuming their dinner meetings and talking foreign policy. And they were headed by none other than Elihu Root, a Nobel laureate and former secretary of state under President Theodore Roosevelt.

Representatives of the Inquiry quickly reassembled and for five months discussed a merger with several members of the defunct New York club. They decided to form a new organization and to restrict membership to U.S. citizens "on the grounds that discussions and other meetings, confidential in nature, would be more productive if participants and speakers knew for sure that the others in the room were all Americans," as Whitney H. Shepardson put it. Shepardson, who was present in Paris as an aide to House and secretary of the commission that drafted the Covenant of the League of Nations, was tasked with telling the British counterparts of the Inquiry that it would no longer be possible to have a joint Anglo-American institute. He was relieved to learn on arriving in London that the British had made the same decision.

Council President John W. Davis, former Secretary of State Elihu Root, Secretary of War Newton Baker, and Foreign Affairs *Editor Hamilton Fish Armstrong*

Back in New York, the original club's members were willing to jettison their name. But, at the last minute, it was decided that calling the new organization the American Institute of International Affairs would wrongly give the impression that it and the similarly named British institution were branches of the same organization. The proposed American Institute of International Affairs was instead called the Council on Foreign Relations.

On July 29, 1921, in the middle of a blistering heat wave in New York City, the Council on Foreign Relations was registered. Its mission would be "to afford a continuous conference on international questions affecting the United States." The Council would pursue its mission in a nonpartisan way, as both Democrats and Republicans were among its founding ranks. It would be an invitation-only membership organization, and its proceedings and events would be closed to the general public, save for rare exceptions.

At the Council's first annual meeting that September, the founding committee was replaced by an elected Board of Directors, which

Two of the Council's founding members: Paul D. Cravath (left) and Edwin F. Gay (right)

then appointed several movers and shakers to lead the organization: Elihu Root was declared the honorary president, giving the organization the instant cachet of having a Nobel laureate on its Board. John W. Davis, a Wall Street lawyer, became president of the Board. A few years later, he aimed for a rather more powerful presidency, running unsuccessfully against Calvin Coolidge in the 1924 national election. Paul D. Cravath, a lawyer and über-manager who developed a set of principles on recruiting, training, compensation, and partnerships that leading law firms across the world would eventually embrace (and call the Cravath System), became the Council's vice president. Edwin F. Gay, a former dean of Harvard's Graduate School of Business Administration and president of the *New York Evening Post*, became secretary and treasurer.

Despite the flashy biographies of its members, many of whom were well off, the Council did not have much money in the early days; instead, it had a different kind of currency—the contacts and networks of its people. These connections allowed them to handpick members

who would further the Council's mission, including university professors and journalists, who were invited to join at rates that were more
in line with what their salaries could afford. Annual dues were $15 for
academics and writers, $50 for members under thirty-five, and $100
for everyone else.

To keep operating costs down, the Council rented just two rooms
on West 43rd Street, enough to accommodate a few desks for staff and
to host small meetings. Only a fraction of the two hundred members
could attend any given event. But when it came to spending social and
political capital, the officers and directors spared no expense.

FIRST STEPS

Georges Clemenceau, the French wartime prime minister, had come to the United States at the Council's invitation, and his trip culminated in a speech before an audience of four thousand at the Metropolitan Opera House on November 21, 1922. In those days, "the old Met" was located in New York's Garment District in a yellow-brick, Italian Renaissance–style building that was demolished in the 1960s, when the city was less careful about preserving its past.

Clemenceau spoke for an hour and a half in English littered with loosely translated French idioms, reminding the audience that he knew America well, having lived in the country just after the close of the Civil War. "Now, I am not going to ask you for money," he told the audience, to raucous laughter. "I want something much more valuable. I want yourself, your heart, your soul." He asked the United States not to turn its back on the League, its friends in Europe, and the efforts that won the war. He asked the United States to prevent Germany from rearming and to pressure Berlin to fulfill the terms of the Paris Peace Conference and the Treaty of Versailles and pay war reparations that were in serious arrears. "We are not looking for trouble. We are merely seeking to put ourselves in a position where we can be assured that we will not be forced into another such terrible war as that we have been through. I think we are entitled to that."

The French statesman's visit generated a lot of press for the Council, but, beyond his audience of internationalists, much of the American public was indifferent to France and the rest of the world. Council members who hoped for a more engaged, proactive, even interventionist foreign policy were disappointed at America's rejection of

Georges Clemenceau (second from right) during his visit to New York City in 1922. Future Foreign Affairs Editor Hamilton Fish Armstrong is on the far left.

international cooperation. As *Foreign Affairs* Editor William G. Hyland wrote in 1992, "They believed that one reason for the turn against Wilsonian internationalism was public ignorance not only about the League but about international affairs in general." Looking back on the 1920s during his 1959 retirement dinner, Walter H. Mallory, the Council's executive director, pointed to the Council's original veterans seated around the room: "Mark them well, for they were on the firing line at a time when internationalism was a bad word, and when anyone who favored the League of Nations was regarded either a Wilsonian Democrat or a crackpot. Since I am not a Democrat, I must myself have been in the latter category."

The directors of the Council were conscious of the responsibilities CFR ought to undertake for the United States to play an expanded role in the world. They understood that fostering informed discussions on foreign policy and educating the broader public on the conduct of international affairs was no small task and that it would not be enough to have small, quiet dinners or the occasional high-profile

The old Metropolitan Opera House in New York, site of the first large CFR meeting in 1922

event, so they included in the Council program a repertoire of activities beyond meetings and conferences.

By 1923, the first study groups were launched to research crucial diplomatic matters. These led to the publication of books and articles intended to inform policymakers: "Postwar Financial and Economic Problems," "Dangerous Areas in Europe," and "The Division Between the Internal and External Concerns of a State: Tradition and Recent Practice of American Diplomacy in This Regard." In 1927, the Council published its broadly focused *Political Handbook of the World.* The annual handbook was meant to be a reference guide to policymakers, diplomats, and academics—a place to look up information about treaties and statistics about countries. It was not retired until 1983. In 1928, the Council published its annual *Survey of American Foreign Relations,* a series that would continue until 1931.

Of all the Council's early initiatives, the creation of *Foreign Affairs* in 1922 is particularly notable. Upon becoming secretary and treasurer, Gay urged the Council to start publishing a journal, and he

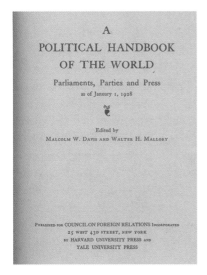

(Left) 1928 edition of A Political Handbook of the World, *which the Council began publishing regularly in 1934; (right) Archibald Cary Coolidge, the first editor of* Foreign Affairs

presided over the Committee on Publication, which explored the best way to do this. He believed a quarterly journal—rather than a weekly or monthly periodical—would allow the Council to maintain the highest quality.

A quarterly called the *Journal of International Relations* was already in circulation, and Gay arranged for its editor, Professor George H. Blakeslee of Clark University, to transfer future publication rights to the Council. Blakeslee's journal was previously known as the *Journal of Race Development*, founded in 1910. The name raised eyebrows, but the content dealt largely with politics, sociology, and international affairs and included submissions from esteemed professors, including W. E. B. Du Bois, the Harvard-educated Black American philosopher, who wrote to Blakeslee on August 11, 1919, "I am much more interested in the old name than in the new name of your journal; but if I have any articles that I think may interest you, I shall be glad indeed to send them."

Gay's strategy was clever. The agreement with the *Journal of International Relations* was less a merger and more a tactic to remove any possible competition. *Foreign Affairs* now needed to find talented editors.

Gay turned to his personal connections and approached Archibald Cary Coolidge, a colleague at Harvard who had been part of the Paris Peace delegation, to become the magazine's editor. As a scholar of

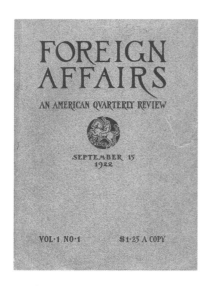

The first edition of Foreign Affairs, September 1922

Russian studies, Coolidge's heart was in research, and he did not find the idea of moving to New York to sit in an office highly appealing. He agreed to oversee the magazine from Cambridge as long as it had a small endowment to sustain publication until revenue started flowing from subscriptions and advertisements. Elihu Root obliged and wrote a check for $25,000. Coolidge also needed a managing editor who would do the day-to-day work in New York. It is unclear whether Coolidge wanted a workhorse or someone too young to outshine him; either way, an outstanding candidate was identified in Hamilton Fish Armstrong, a history professor also at Harvard who was twenty-nine years old and full of creative energy.

The first issue of *Foreign Affairs* went to press in the fall of 1922 and the following year was hitting newsstands on a quarterly basis. It cost $1.25, a sum that could fill a bag with groceries in those days. Predictably, Elihu Root wrote the lead article, "A Requisite for the Success of Popular Democracy," setting the tone of the mission of the Council and magazine for decades to come: "Without good knowledge of international affairs there can be no good intelligent discussion of foreign policy and diplomatic conduct."

Circulation came close to touching five thousand in the first year, double Armstrong's expectations. There was a sizable core audience with an appetite to understand the world—one that was made up of elite, educated, highly literate readers. The journal's pages displayed an urgency during those first years—preoccupation with war debts, alarm over Germany's militarism, foreboding about Japan's violent expansion in Asia, concern with the state of the world economy and trade, and worries about the future of internationalism. A

Facing page: *Three early authors in* Foreign Affairs: *W. E. B. Du Bois, Leon Trotsky, and Dorothy Thompson*

good number of the articles led with themes and titles that will strike some readers today as familiar: "Our Much-Abused State Department," "Our Mexican Immigrants," "Islam and Britain," and "The Tariff as a Factor in American Foreign Trade."

Coolidge saw the magazine as providing the sole arena for unified discussion of international affairs, and he was careful to point out that he and Armstrong favored writers who brought a wide difference of opinion over dull and useless consensus. He demanded that contributors be competent and well informed. *Foreign Affairs* published articles by Du Bois, who wrote about race and foreign policy; Leon Trotsky, the Bolshevik revolutionary and intellectual who was a close associate of Vladimir Lenin; and Dorothy Thompson, an American columnist who was qualified to publish an early exposé on the danger of Nazi Germany but not qualified for Council membership because of her gender. The magazine, it seemed, was ahead of its time.

By 1927, *Foreign Affairs* had a modest $25,000 reserve, and its circulation had boomed to ten thousand, while the Council had grown respectably to include 391 members, 7 staffers, and a budget of $100,000, the majority coming from membership dues and the sale of publications.

Secretary of State Frank B. Kellogg

The following year, Frank B. Kellogg, CFR member and secretary of state in the Calvin Coolidge administration, headlined a dinner conversation at the Council entitled "The War Prevention Policy of the United States." Months later in Paris, the Kellogg-Briand Pact was born. Signed by the United States, France, and Germany, the pact renounced the use of war as an instrument of policy and called for the peaceful resolution of diplomatic disputes. In the coming months, many states would join the pact, which did little to prevent future wars or the rise of militarism in Europe. Its central provisions, however, would be incorporated later into the charter of the United Nations.

THE GREAT DEPRESSION AND
THE SLIDE TO WAR

By the early 1930s, the Great Depression had devastated the U.S. economy and driven the country into isolation. The Council took a beating as its budget shrank by half and income at *Foreign Affairs* dropped when subscribers stopped renewing. Both the Council and the magazine had to find ways to cut costs, and the Board of Directors appealed to members to help in CFR's 1933–34 Annual Report: "It is hoped that any member who has not subscribed to the fund, but who can possibly do so, will come forward to help in maintaining the high standard which *Foreign Affairs* has set in its field." Council members gave what they could to keep the organization afloat, even as many found their own fortunes endangered.

Despite the economic stressors of the time, nerves rarely frayed at Council events, and disagreements were typically cordial. A March 1933 event was a notable exception. The Council had invited a Japanese diplomat to explain Japan's war on China and its invasion of Manchuria. This infuriated U.S. Secretary of State and CFR member Henry L. Stimson, who was aghast that "the Council on Foreign Relations, with its extremely high though unofficial standing, should lend itself to furthering the subversive effects of such propaganda. . . . The Council existed for a rather more responsible purpose." This was certainly not the last time a speaker generated controversy, and episodically over the decades Council members would object to an invited speaker. But early on, such events gave leadership the opportunity to be clear about the Council's policy: CFR was open to hearing a broad variety of views, even unpopular ones, and under no circumstances should anyone confuse a speaker's presence or a comment made at a Council event as the position of the organization.

By 1933, a quarter of Americans were out of work due to the Great Depression.

Still, Stimson's objections over the speaker were an unexpected challenge. In *The Wise Men of Foreign Affairs: The History of the Council on Foreign Relations*, Robert D. Schulzinger explained how the Council moved to contain the damage: "Stimson was too import-ant for CFR to drop, so they invited him to join the editorial board of *Foreign Affairs*, made him chairman on a [study] group on the Philippines, but kept him off the Board of Directors." The move to soothe Stimson was smart, if inappropriate by the standards of the twenty-first century. Today, no government official would be given editorial oversight over *Foreign Affairs*.

Meanwhile, Hamilton Fish Armstrong used his editorial perch at *Foreign Affairs* to sound the alarm over rising militarism and nationalism in Europe. He became the chief editor after Coolidge died in 1928, and he was determined to take the magazine to greater heights. To do so, he traveled extensively and was, according to a 1971 *New York Times* piece,

A 1933 speech at CFR by Japanese diplomat Yosuke Matsuoka (left) infuriated Secretary of State Henry L. Stimson (right).

. . . more likely to be found in Paris or Vienna than in his New York office. . . . In an age in which isolationism was rampant in the United States and newspaper coverage of international affairs scanty and often mediocre, Armstrong went abroad in order to study critical situations first-hand and also to persuade leading figures in the world of diplomacy to write articles for *Foreign Affairs* about the problems with which they were wrestling.

In April 1933, Armstrong secured an interview with Adolf Hitler, who had become chancellor of Germany earlier that year. Armstrong recounted in his book *Peace and Counter-Peace: From Wilson to Hitler* how Hitler subjected him to an unending and abusive monologue about neighboring Poland and insisted on Germany's right to rearm. When Hitler dismissed him, Armstrong resolved to pay him back for the awful lecture "and thanked him 'for addressing me alone when

A Nazi rally in Germany around 1934. Hamilton Fish Armstrong cautioned about Hitler's rise.

usually he addressed sixty million.'" Hitler took this sarcasm as a compliment. In *Continuing the Inquiry*, Peter Grose wrote,

> The young editor emerged from the Berlin chancellery deeply shocked at the values and goals conveyed to him with a demagoguery that the world at large would eventually come to know all too well. He opened his journal to authors who could dissect the looming Nazi phenomenon with more pointed expertise than his own.

Sufficiently concerned with the rise of militarism in Europe and Asia, the Council's Board scraped together funds in 1936 to organize the first of its Conferences for University Men, events that brought next-generation scholars together with senior experts to discuss international affairs. The first of these tackled the subject of neutrality and sanctions, which were being hotly debated in the wake of Japan's occupation of Manchuria and Italy's invasion of

Ethiopia. Senior undergradu-
ates, PhD students, and young
faculty from northeastern universities shared the table with
Thomas W. Lamont of J.P.
Morgan and Allen W. Dulles, a
lawyer who wrote about sanctions and would later enter U.S.
government service to become
the longest-serving director of
central intelligence. These conferences were a tentative foray
into education and outreach,
initiatives that have become a
mainstay of the Council in the
twenty-first century.

Brooks Emeny of the Cleveland committee was an early proponent of CFR's national expansion.

The following year, the Carnegie Corporation stepped in with
a $50,000 grant that enabled the Council to set up Committees on
Foreign Relations in eight American cities, mostly in the Midwest.
The committees were largely autonomous in their day-to-day affairs,
but the Council saw them as a way to bring together "local gentlemen
of influence" to organize discussions of American foreign policy in
their own communities. These committees occasionally served as a
way to recruit members who lived outside New York, but, for the most
part, committee participants were not Council members.

The relationship between the Council and the committees was
occasionally turbulent, and CFR officers were quick to step in when
they felt the committees were overstepping their bounds. Walter
Mallory insisted "that the Committees should not be 'action groups'
sponsoring particular policies, but should serve only for the enlight-
enment" of those who belonged to them.

In late 1941, Brooks Emeny, the director of Cleveland's Committee on Foreign Relations, approached the Carnegie Corporation
for money to expand the nationwide committees. Leadership at the
Council exploded in anger and moved to quash any funding. Russell C. Leffingwell, partner at J.P. Morgan and CFR Board member,
huffed that "miscellaneous chatter about foreign affairs is likely to do
more harm than good." It would take another half century before the
Council resolved its relationship with the committees.

A SECOND WORLD WAR AND ITS AFTERMATH

On September 1, 1939, Germany invaded Poland. Armstrong telephoned his contacts in the State Department and suggested that the Council pitch in to help with policy planning for the looming war. Armstrong and Mallory traveled to Washington, DC, and met with George S. Messersmith, assistant secretary of state in the Franklin D. Roosevelt administration. Armstrong and Mallory proposed that the Council put together a series of independent study groups to inform and guide American foreign policy for the coming conflict and to provide policy advice for the postwar world.

The State Department was far smaller in those days, operating with a constrained budget and, until 1947, without a policy planning staff. A Council monograph on the initiative, *The War and Peace Studies of the Council on Foreign Relations, 1939–1945*, explained,

> There was no doubt that even if the United States avoided being drawn into the war, its interests would become profoundly engaged as the conflict progressed; and certainly they would be directly affected by the eventual peace settlements. The Council representatives suggested that, particularly pending the time when the Department itself was able to assemble staff and begin research and analysis on a proper scale, the Council might undertake work in certain specific fields, without, of course, any formal assignment of responsibility on the one side or restriction of independent action on the other.

This made the Council's offer appealing.

People in Washington, DC, reading about the German invasion of Poland, 1939

With the State Department's quiet agreement and a sizable $350,000 grant from the Rockefeller Foundation (over $4 million in 2021 dollars), the War and Peace Studies project was born. It was a beast of a project, crowded with nearly one hundred experts and personalities that needed to be managed, a job that Percy W. Bidwell, the Council's first director of Studies, performed well. The experts were divided into thematic groups: Security and Armaments, Economic and Financial Issues, Politics, Territorial, and Peace Aims. Over the course of five years, the experts took part in 362 meetings and produced 682 memos for the State Department.

The Armaments group, which Allen Dulles led, was compelling. It did not get much attention until the United States started to win the war and State Department planners realized they needed a plan for the occupation of Germany. The Office of Strategic Services would later recruit Dulles to implement the plan. A group working on East Asia included Owen Lattimore, a brilliant sinologist with leftist sympathies who advocated for the State Department to avoid adopting policies that needlessly harmed Communist China. Lattimore's work had

U.S. Navy ships in Greenland during World War II

an ideological edge—one that got him into trouble in the McCarthy era—but his expertise was hard to ignore when setting policy.

Isaiah Bowman's Territorial group examined strategic considerations regarding nonstate territories, gray zones, and colonial holdings. This was a period in history when the number of sovereign states was significantly smaller, and European countries and the United States controlled vast colonies and territories. (During its short life span, the League of Nations had 63 members, whereas the United Nations today has 193 member states.) Bowman's group generated 128 documents and memos. Among them was one that had an unexpected impact.

On March 17, 1940, a confidential memo from Bowman's group pointed out the strategic importance of Greenland to transatlantic aviation. Greenland was a Danish colony and ran the risk of being occupied if Germany were to overrun Denmark. The group suggested that the United States declare Greenland part of the Monroe Doctrine's geographical space. Soon after dispatching the report, Bowman was summoned to the White House. According to CFR's

Members of the Advisory Committee on Refugees Hamilton Fish Armstrong, Sumner Welles, George Warren, and James G. McDonald exiting the White House

1947 anniversary book, "President Roosevelt had a copy of the memorandum in his hand and turned to his visitor for advice because of his part in raising the question of Greenland's strategic importance." When Nazi Germany invaded Denmark a few weeks later, Roosevelt promptly organized a press conference announcing Greenland as part of the North American continent. Months before Germany declared war on the United States, the Danish government-in-exile granted Roosevelt the right to build bases and radar facilities in Greenland.

War and Peace Studies attracted some contemporaneous detractors, including those who saw the work as, *The Wise Men of Foreign Affairs* recorded, "about as relevant as last year's almanac." Historians could argue that the people who led the work overstated their influence. Impact, after all, is notoriously difficult to gauge, leaving only counterfactuals about what might have happened if War and Peace Studies had never come about. Would the Nazis have overrun Greenland? Would the occupation of a defeated Germany look fundamentally different? It is impossible to know with certainty.

Allied troops landing in Normandy on D-Day, June 6, 1944

What is clear is that the group that made up the War and Peace Studies project faced a much more collaborative, forward-looking administration with a global outlook than did the scholars of the Inquiry in the 1920s.

On the eve of World War II, before Japanese planes bombed Pearl Harbor, the State Department was short-staffed and beleaguered, its budget decimated by the brutal Depression. The hand that the Council extended was eagerly grasped.

THE COUNCIL FINDS A HOME

April 6, 1945—The war was not yet over, but an end was in sight. Nazi forces were on the retreat throughout Europe, and the Japanese were intensifying kamikaze attacks on American naval forces. In a muted ceremony on New York's Upper East Side, Hamilton Armstrong and Russell Leffingwell, the Council s new chair of the Board of Directors, stood alongside U.S. Secretary of State and CFR member Edward Stettinius as the Harold Pratt House was opened.

The elegant five-story mansion was a gift to the Council by Harriet Barnes Pratt in memory of her husband, Harold, who had been among the Council's earliest members. Harold Irving Pratt was the director of Standard Oil of New Jersey, which had been acquired by the Rockefeller family. Harriet Pratt's only condition was that the Board raise the necessary funds for upkeep; John D. Rockefeller Jr. led an enthusiastic group of two hundred members who pledged the money. Believing the house to be far too large for her, she hoped the Council would make the most of its warm spaces, including the oak reception room and its fireplace, which she adored. In a letter to Walter Mallory, she suggested how the Council might furnish the room and design shelves to display CFR's work. "There is no more beautiful and no more satisfactory wallpaper than books," she wrote. "Periodicals lack charm."

The gift gave the Council room to work and grow. Since its inception, the Council had moved from a two-room office to a modest brownstone. The year before Pratt House was dedicated, the Council was bursting at the seams. It had twenty full-time researchers, not including support staff; the library could barely contain its twenty-four thousand books; and meeting space was limited, making it impossible to accommodate all members who wanted to participate in events.

The Harold Pratt House at the time it was donated to the Council

The first speaker at the Pratt House was Secretary of State Edward Stettinius (second from right), shown here with (left to right) John W. Davis, Russell C. Leffingwell, and Hamilton Fish Armstrong.

Pratt's generosity gave the Council the gift of space in a crowded and expensive city—space that allowed its officers, staff, and members to make the most of its mission in the decades that followed.

By the Council's twenty-fifth anniversary in 1946, fifty-five officers had served on its Board. Of these, thirty-five were Ivy League graduates, and three had studied at Oxford University. As Grose detailed in *Continuing the Inquiry*:

> Lawyers from the Wall Street firms predominated in the occupational grouping; the 55 Council officers and directors also held 74 corporate directorships. Next came professional academics, with five university presidents. . . . Twelve of the leadership had served in cabinet or subcabinet positions for different administrations in the interwar and wartime years; another 30 had experience elsewhere in the federal bureaucracy, including 21 in

the State Department. A typical Council officer belonged to three social clubs from a list of 170; the Century and Knickerbocker in New York and the Cosmos and Metropolitan in Washington were the most popular.

These numbers and the earlier fight with the Cleveland committee revealed a lot about the Council in this period. Although it was open to debate and new thinking in foreign policy, it was a guarded membership organization and zealously defended its role. The majority of its members and officers lived and worked in New York, with a smaller core residing in Washington, DC, or shuttling between the two cities. It was an elite, northeastern institution, overwhelmingly white and exclusively male. Membership meant an audience with policymakers and economic titans at dinner events; participation in the study groups that formed the core of the Council's work meant access to power and the possibility to shape the course of U.S. foreign policy.

FROM WORLD WAR TO COLD WAR

The interviewer leaned in to ask, "If you hadn't been part of the 1956 study group at the Council, how would your professional life have differed?"

"Well," Henry Kissinger replied after the briefest hesitation, "my plan was to write a history of the building of the international system in the nineteenth century and its collapse. This was supposed to be the first, and the outbreak of World War I would have been the [last]. In between, I was going to write a book on Bismarck and a number of other books. This is a very instructive period if you're interested in diplomacy."

Kissinger had no route to a career in government service, let alone a plan for becoming secretary of state. He would have been content to remain a Harvard professor. But the Council study group on nuclear weapons and foreign policy in 1956 altered his course.

"The Council was a seminal shaping experience in my life," Kissinger said as the interview came to a close. "It introduced me to a world that seemed totally remote from me. Had I not wound up with the study group at the Council, I would have been a historian."

Kissinger's story speaks to the Council's influence and role in the years that followed World War II, when America became a superpower and the Cold War brought new and unfamiliar challenges. From the mid-1940s to the late 1960s, the Council broadened the scope of its work beyond the conventional list of foreign policy subjects to include the control of nuclear weapons, the rise of development assistance, international cultural cooperation, and decolonization. The Council's work in these areas created opportunities for a younger generation to join the ranks of the policymaking establishment and shape American foreign policy, and Kissinger's story is the ultimate example of the

George C. Marshall (left) and George F. Kennan (right)

Council fostering a career in public service. The Council was at the height of its influence, even though tougher times were on the horizon.

• • •

The year 1947 defined the postwar era. President Harry S. Truman's Secretary of State George C. Marshall called for a sweeping program of economic aid to rebuild Europe. The Marshall Plan was driven by the fear of communist expansion in war-ravaged Western Europe, which faced little prospect of economic recovery. The plan revived Western Europe's economies, created markets for American exports, precluded cooperation with the Soviet bloc, and tightened the bond across the Atlantic.

It was the beginning of the era of containment, a policy that became the foundation of the Truman administration's approach to the Soviet Union, constituted the baseline strategy that the United States used throughout the Cold War, and came to light in the pages of *Foreign Affairs* when the magazine published an article by George

An atomic bomb test on Bikini Atoll, 1946

F. Kennan, the architect of containment, who was working quietly as a State Department expert on Russia.

Kennan might have remained unknown to the American public had it not been for George S. Franklin. Franklin had been hired to work on a study group on U.S.-Soviet relations in 1945, the same year American B-29s dropped atomic bombs on Hiroshima and Nagasaki, killing tens of thousands of people in the initial blasts, bringing an end to the war in the Pacific, accelerating the Soviet Union's nuclear program, and fueling debates in the pages of *Foreign Affairs* on the existential dangers of war and the need for arms control. Hanson W. Baldwin, a military correspondent, wrote in October 1945 that America's use of atomic weapons "marked the first harnessing of the sun's power on a large scale, with all the untold consequences for good and evil implicit in the achievement." Humanity had developed the means to destroy itself.

Although the Soviet Union would not test its first atomic weapon until 1949, Franklin's study group faced a more immediate task—how to cooperate with the Soviet Union to further America's interests in Europe and around the world. Franklin did his best to channel the dozens of experts in the group to a productive discussion. Consensus could not be reached, and Franklin tried to split the difference in his draft report: "Cooperation between the U.S. and the Soviet Union is as essential as almost anything in the world today. . . . Cooperation, however, does not mean that we should knuckle under, or allow ourselves to become weak." Frank Altschul, an American financier and Council Board member, savaged the draft, arguing that the time for negotiation and compromise with the Soviet Union was over. Isaiah Bowman dealt the report a fatal blow, telling Franklin it contained nothing "fresh . . . excellent or useful" for scholars or policymakers. The report was buried unpublished in Council archives.

Instead of losing his job, Franklin was promoted to lead the Council's Meetings Program (he eventually became executive director in 1953, a role similar to that of today's president) and in January 1947 attended a small meeting at which he heard George Kennan talk about Russia. Franklin was riveted and, being well informed on U.S.-Soviet relations, recognized talent when he saw it. He reflected in 1960, "I immediately sent some notes I had taken to Ham Armstrong, suggesting that Kennan write an article based on the talk he had given." Armstrong agreed and roped Kennan in to write what became the most influential article *Foreign Affairs* published in the Cold War years, "The Sources of Soviet Conduct." Published in July 1947, authorship was attributed to "X," as neither Kennan nor the State Department wanted attribution. Kennan was self-effacing, insisting that he had nothing useful to contribute. He also gave up his original, rather awkward title, "The Psychological Background of Soviet Foreign Policy."

The article was electrifying. Kennan summarized three hundred years of Russian history to make the point that a legacy of imperial expansion, not communist ideology, guided Soviet actions. Rooted in the classified "Long Telegram" that Kennan had written months earlier to the secretary of state, his *Foreign Affairs* article argued that the USSR would eventually collapse under the weight of its internal contradictions and the United States did not need to confront it; instead, the United States could wait it out with a containment strategy. "The main element of any United States policy toward the Soviet Union," he explained, "must be that of a long-term, patient but firm and vigilant containment of Russian expansive tendencies." Containment, he predicted, would encourage "either the break-up or the gradual mellowing of Soviet power."

In closing, Kennan added a flourish likely intended for the broader American public:

To avoid destruction the United States need only measure up to its own best traditions and prove itself worthy of preservation as a great nation. Surely, there was never a fairer test of national quality than this. In the light of these circumstances, the thoughtful observer of Russian-American relations will find no cause for complaint in the Kremlin's challenge to American society. He will rather experience a certain gratitude to a Providence which, by providing the American people with this implacable challenge, has made their entire security as a nation dependent on their pulling themselves together and accepting the responsibilities of moral and political leadership that history plainly intended them to bear.

Writing has changed much since those days, and it is unlikely that today's editors at the Council or *Foreign Affairs* would print such prose. As Peter Grose, historian and former managing editor of the magazine, put it, "This is the way people talked and wrote in those days. Yes, it was messianic. Kennan was messianic. Everybody was. And his point was, 'Don't worry. The Russians are not supermen. They're not going to take us over.' The rest, it's colorful rhetoric."

The Kennan episode was the most public example of the Council in action—tackling new subjects and catapulting writers and hidden experts to fame. Fareed Zakaria, who decades later would become managing editor of *Foreign Affairs* and go on to host CNN's *Fareed Zakaria GPS*, explains,

> It is one thing to have George Kennan write for you when he's George Kennan the famous diplomat scholar. It is another to have him when he's an obscure diplomat.... A well-run magazine that has confidence in itself will look for young people who are writing brilliant stuff and then make them famous.

And in this period, the Council and its magazine were treading new ground while fueling the careers of such talents as Kennan and Kissinger.

The same year that *Foreign Affairs* published Kennan, the Council held a series of general meetings and discussion groups on the emerging Marshall Plan. The U.S. Congress approved the plan in March 1948, funneling $12 billion over time to rebuild Europe. The architects of the plan included Council members Dean Acheson, soon-to-be

*Dwight D. Eisenhower on the steps of
Columbia University*

Truman's secretary of state and architect of postwar institutions such as NATO and the International Monetary Fund; William Clayton, the first undersecretary for economic affairs; and George Kennan. The plan had many enthusiastic supporters among Council members and directors, including Allen Dulles, who had become president of CFR's Board in 1946.

This did not mean that the Council's 1947 Marshall Plan study group would give the plan an easy pass. The group asked tough questions: Would the plan allow Europeans to stand on their own feet, or would they become hooked on aid? Were there conflicts between strategic and economic goals, and what would it take to make sure that the two moved in lockstep? Was this a job for the State Department or better suited for another agency? And what if the United States did not like the policies Europeans were pursuing? In asking these questions, the group was not looking for consensus; rather, it was making sure the Truman administration had thought through the plan's consequences.

In 1948, George Franklin and Walter Mallory took a short trip from the Upper East Side to Morningside Heights to see the president of Columbia University. They hoped to persuade him to chair a study group on the future of U.S.-European relations that would examine the role of aid and the shaping of a new strategic alliance. The time was right, as the United States and several European countries were in early discussions that ultimately led to the formation of NATO. Some Council officers thought that asking the president of Columbia to do this was overly ambitious, but in half an hour Mallory and Franklin convinced him to sign up. And with that, General Dwight D. Eisenhower, president of an Ivy League institution and not yet president of the United States, became chair of the study group. Franklin and

Mallory raced to Penn Station that night and took a train to Detroit. By lunchtime the next day, they had convinced the Ford Foundation to finance the project.

Eisenhower was a "superb chairman," according to Franklin, "drawing out not only the prominent, recognized members of the group like Allen Dulles, David E. Lilienthal, Isidor Rabi, and Jacob Viner, but also brilliant younger men like McGeorge Bundy." The group discussed the implementation of the Marshall Plan and segued into conversation about security strategy in Western Europe. By 1950, Eisenhower had drafted a letter to President Truman, urging him to bolster American forces and arguing that NATO was inadequate to confront the Soviet threat. Alongside Eisenhower's signature were those of twelve other Council members and staff. Truman agreed to deploy 180,000 men, if Eisenhower would accept NATO command.

Another 1948 study group on cultural cooperation and foreign policy met ten times and hosted surprisingly sharp debates, including on the role of the UN Educational, Scientific, and Cultural Organization (UNESCO). American officials wanted to use the UN agency to oppose the Soviet Union on matters of education, while NATO allies such as France and Italy preferred a more conciliatory approach. UNESCO's preamble—"wars begin in the minds of men"—signaled that culture, education, and ideology were also going to become vicious Cold War battlegrounds.

The same year, a study group with the clunky title "U.S. Policy Toward Non-Self-Governing Territories" debated the legacy of colonization. The issue was pressing, since half a billion people in India, Indonesia, and elsewhere had become or were on the cusp of becoming independent. Members of the group did not spare the United States criticism usually reserved for colonial powers such as Britain and France. The United States, after all, had held on to the Philippines until 1946 and was still in possession of territories such as Puerto Rico and a multitude of islands in the South Pacific. The report concluded, "In the eyes of the world, the United States is an imperial power, but neither the American people nor their government admit this to be true."

While some members at Council meetings took policymakers to task for being oblivious to how America was perceived abroad, others tried to project a more benevolent side to America's role and its strategic assistance. That spring, Council members responded to a request from the Rockefeller Foundation to aid Japan by stocking the library of the Diet with books and periodicals—as a defeated power, Japan was

The Akasaka Detached Palace in Tokyo, home to Japan's National Diet Library

under the authority of the supreme commander of the Allied Powers until 1952. A group of Council members worked with the Council's assistant librarian to select, purchase, and ship 2,629 social science titles. At the time, the Council had one of the best reference libraries on foreign policy in the United States.

MASS MEDIA AND
MASSIVE RETALIATION

Americans in record numbers had switched off their radios and turned on new television sets to get their news and relax after a day's work. On January 12, 1954, this created a unique opportunity for the Council when it hosted John Foster Dulles—a long-serving Council member, now President Eisenhower's secretary of state—for a televised address on American foreign policy. Not since Clemenceau's speech at the old Met in 1922 had the Council made such an important break in its tradition of off-the-record meetings.

The decision to broadcast the event reflected a shift toward television by political elites eager to reach the American public, including Wisconsin Senator Joseph McCarthy, who made a political career out of persecuting Americans, among them several Council members, for alleged communist sympathies. McCarthy had already taken to the airwaves to accuse Eisenhower of treasonously failing to purge the government of gays and communists.

Dulles used the televised address to lay out the administration's new security strategy against the Soviet Union. His introduction was tame: "First of all, let us recognize that many of the preceding foreign policies were good." He went on to mention the Marshall Plan, the role of the United Nations in the Korean War, and the buildup of conventional forces in Europe. But the Soviets, as he and Eisenhower saw it, were maneuvering globally, expanding their influence, and compelling the United States to deploy troops permanently in Asia.

Dulles believed that the Truman administration had been too permissive toward the Soviet Union. His speech signaled a recalibration of foreign policy and reflected Eisenhower's desire to rein in the defense budget; both the president and Dulles saw atomic weapons

Members of the Council attending the dinner with John Foster Dulles, January 1954

as a more effective deterrent against communist aggression and less expensive than large-scale troop deployments. Dulles summed it up, "We want, for ourselves and the other free nations, a maximum deterrent at a bearable cost."

Dulles's speech was hugely important in rolling out a policy of massive retaliation, clarifying containment, and delivering the message that Soviet aggression would be met with a painful response "instantly, by means and at places of our choosing." As Mira Rapp-Hooper, CFR Stephen A. Schwarzman senior fellow for Asia studies, explained in a conversation with George Gavrilis on July 27, 2020, "There was little ambiguity in that message. In rolling it out, Dulles made it clear in the most public, high-profile way that his escalatory policy would apply to aggression against U.S. allies as well. And in using the Council with all its stature, convening power, and connections to the policy elite to make his case publicly, Dulles sent an unmistakable signal to the Soviets."

NUCLEAR WEAPONS AND
FOREIGN POLICY

On a Friday in 1955, Henry Kissinger ran into Arthur Schlesinger Jr. in Harvard Yard. Schlesinger was a Council member and an award-winning professor of American history who was writing about the Truman administration. Kissinger was a young junior professor studying diplomacy and strategy but had not yet written his first policy article. Schlesinger showed him a letter from Thomas K. Finletter, secretary of the air force in the Truman administration and future U.S. ambassador to NATO, explaining the intricacies of massive retaliation. Kissinger later wrote to Schlesinger, laying out his own views against massive retaliation, and Schlesinger shared this note with Armstrong at *Foreign Affairs*.

Armstrong promptly asked Kissinger to flesh out his views in an article. Kissinger's first *Foreign Affairs* piece led to another opportunity at the Council when Franklin asked him to serve as secretary of a new study group, "Nuclear Weapons and Foreign Policy." The Council was eager to assess America's nuclear strategy, and Schlesinger, along with a few other Council members who spanned the political spectrum, felt the young professor would serve the study group well as its rapporteur.

Kissinger later joked about the occasion, "In those days, I was even more arrogant. I said, 'I don't work as secretary. I will write the report in my own hand or I won't do it, but of course I'll use the study group and play by its rules.' That created a conflict with Paul Nitze, who thought he might be the chief figure and that I'd be his assistant." Kissinger promptly became the leader and rapporteur of the study group.

The first meeting opened a door to a new world. Kissinger explained, "I had done some very low-level consulting drudgework for

Hardcover edition of the unexpected best-selling CFR book Nuclear Weapons and Foreign Policy *by Henry Kissinger*

the Operations Research Office, which was sort of an ad corporation for the army. I'd done some minor-league things like this, but here I was meeting the really top people in their field, and the Council at that time had a monopoly." Kissinger ran the meetings and shaped the discussions. He even had the opportunity to visit Princeton University and spend the day with J. Robert Oppenheimer, the acclaimed physicist who oversaw the effort to develop atomic weapons.

Despite the huge importance of the subject, Kissinger did not recall acrimonious arguments. The distinguished group he led was much more concerned with devising an alternative to massive retaliation.

Once in a while, there were animated discussions. Mervin Kelly, a physicist, engineer, and director of Bell Telephone Laboratories, insisted that intercontinental missiles were not viable because propulsion required so much fuel that there would not be room for warheads.

The study group concluded that massive retaliation had to be supplanted with a more realistic and flexible strategy, one that acknowledged the possibility that the United States and the Soviet Union could fight a limited war in which tactical nuclear weapons would likely be used along with conventional forces.

The Council published Kissinger's book *Nuclear Weapons and Foreign Policy* in June 1957 as a culmination of his work with the study group. "It was a stunning surprise when my book became a best seller," Kissinger explained. "That was not the intention." The book placed him in the national spotlight, and his future as national security advisor, secretary of state, and global statesman was set into motion.

If influence is defined as the ability to create leaders and statesmen or the capacity to shape debates on what is and is not possible in international affairs, the Council could be described as the most influential or predominant institution of international affairs in the 1950s. And *Foreign Affairs* did its part serving policymakers and the educated public with good, solid, and sober articles on foreign policy. Armstrong offered the following explanation:

> Of course the fundamental change for American diplomacy was that this time the American people as a whole, looking at the world with eyes opened by a second terrible experience, saw that their interests and responsibilities reached to every part of it. This meant that their leaders could enter without hesitation into a policy of active international cooperation; and with the public behind them, they did so. . . . Without steady public backing, a Truman, Eisenhower, or Kennedy could not have pursued a strong foreign policy, and if he had tried would have ended like Wilson in frustration.

Foreign Affairs' circulation jumped from 19,110 in 1950 to 47,000 in 1962. It was just one of many signs of the coming of age of a superpower, an America that was decidedly internationalist in its outlook.

Following pages: Command post of U.S. Air Force Strategic Air Command, 1947

46

THE COUNCIL PIVOTS TO ASIA

The year 1962 had been eventful around much of the world, with episodes cascading in short order, some hopeful and others harrowing. Decolonization in Africa was moving fast. In the United States, where John F. Kennedy was now president, federal marshals escorted the first Black student at the University of Mississippi as he registered for classes, a sign of how far the country still had to go to achieve racial equality. The Cuban Missile Crisis, brief as it was, struck fear into the hearts of millions of Americans, who wondered if their lives could end in a nuclear cloud. And a band of British lads called the Rolling Stones made their debut in a small London club.

It was a somewhat quiet year at the Council, where staff were busy with new initiatives. The Council secured a large grant from the Ford Foundation to inaugurate two new Studies programs. The first, Atlantic Policy Studies, would publish a number of works, including in 1965 Zbigniew Brzezinski's *Alternative to Partition: For a Broader Conception of America's Role in Europe*. Brzezinski, a Council member and professor of international affairs at Columbia University, had advised the Kennedy and Lyndon B. Johnson presidential campaigns to build political and economic relations with Eastern Europe and a policy of détente with the Soviet Union. The year after Brzezinski's book came out, President Johnson appointed him to the Policy Planning Council of the State Department.

The second initiative, The United States and China in World Affairs, signaled the Council's growing attention to Asia, despite political sensitivities. George Franklin recalls that the Ford Foundation practically forced grant money on the Council, arguing that the United States was "blind" to alternative ways to forge relations with Communist China.

Rural rally in support of the Chinese Communist Party, early 1950s

Franklin agreed. "I thought that it was a good idea since China policy had been stuck in the mud and was regarded as so politically sensitive that it was almost impossible to discuss alternatives to it."

Wounds were still fresh from the acrimonious debates on who should be blamed for China's going communist in 1949. During China's Civil War, when much of the country was under Japanese occupation, the United States had provided aid to Chiang Kai-shek's Nationalist Party and tried to negotiate a peace agreement between the Nationalists and Mao Zedong's Communist forces. Once Japan's armed forces in China surrendered on September 2, 1945, the two factions resumed fighting, and the tide eventually turned in the Communists' favor. On March 30, 1950, the year after the People's Republic of China was formed, Senator McCarthy had gone on a rampage against the Truman and Eisenhower administrations: "It was not Chinese democracy under Mao that conquered China as Acheson, Lattimore, and Jessup contended. Soviet Russia conquered China, and an important ally of this conqueror was the small left-wing element in our Department of State."

Over a decade later, the United States had no diplomatic relations with China, and advocating for relations remained politically risky. Certain voices at the Council opposed the program, and they pointed out that the Institute of Pacific Relations had been devastated when donors pulled their support as soon as it started to discuss scenarios for U.S.-China relations. Grayson Kirk, president of Columbia University and soon-to-be CFR's Board president, felt differently. He argued that the time had come to reevaluate policy toward China, and the Council decided to move ahead with the program. As it turned out, one of the books that came out of the initiative found that the educated American public was not against rethinking relations with Communist China. The American people, it seemed, were ahead of their government.

GOOD FELLOWSHIP

I n the first part of the 1960s, the Council experimented with a series of fellowship programs, designed to bring practitioners and experts on international relations to the Pratt House to study particular foreign policies, military strategies, or countries considered essential to the United States. In 1962, the air force fellowship was created for service members who wanted to spend time at the Council studying policy. In 1966, the army fellowship was added, along with the Murrow fellowship for visiting journalists, thanks to a grant from the CBS Foundation. Thereafter, the navy asked the Council to create a fellowship for its members, and the Council obliged. But of all the fellowship programs the Council created, the most consequential was given the vaguest name: the International Affairs Fellowship.

Some Council staff, including George Franklin and Director of Administration John Temple Swing, were quietly worried. The Council's officers were aging; Whitney Shepardson, for instance, had been present at the Inquiry and a member of the Board since the Council's creation. Membership too was getting older; the average age was approaching sixty, threatening to antiquate the Council. "Something had to be done to bring in new blood to the Council," Swing explained, a worry that in 1966 led to the creation of the International Affairs Fellowship program. This would become the Council's hallmark fellowship program, bridging the gap between the study and the making of U S. foreign policy and creating the next generation of scholar-practitioners.

The program had an interesting start when James Hyde dropped in on George Franklin. Hyde was a program officer at the Rockefeller Brothers Fund and told Franklin that he was going to phase out a

fellowship for young academics. Hyde wondered whether the Council could pick up the baton. Franklin's initial reaction was to decline the offer: "We're not a university; we don't have graduate students. What comparative advantage could we possibly have to run what is in essence a graduate program?" But Swing stepped in, saying, "George, let's not say no just yet. Let's go back and think how we could use this program to our advantage and still serve some of the purposes that the Rockefeller Brothers Fund wanted to have." It helped that Hyde was offering the Council $300,000 to take on the fellowship.

Swing got to work tailoring the program to the Council's mission. The program would focus on young academics, but it would not be a typical sabbatical to write a book on the way to tenure. "It would be different in that we would try to get academics out of the ivory tower and into policy positions for a year in Washington with the National Security Council staff, or whatever staff it would be," Swing said. The idea was viable; the Council had excellent connections with the U.S. government.

The International Affairs Fellowship kicked off with a pilot in 1966 and was formally launched in 1967. Among the early fellows were young international relations faculty such as Graham Allison and Robert O. Keohane, who became academic giants in the respective fields of strategic decision-making and international institutions. It was hard work for Swing, who had to identify candidates in their twenties and thirties well before the days of the internet and LinkedIn. "I wrote a letter to the dean of every graduate school in the country that had an international relations program," he reflected.

The effort paid off over the years and launched many careers beyond typical academic orbits. Richard Solomon started his career as a young academic and was planning to use his fellowship in 1971–72 to write a comparative psychohistory of Mao Zedong and Richard M. Nixon. Instead, Swing secured him a spot with the National Security Council just as Nixon was warming up to China. Solomon stayed in government service and eventually became assistant secretary of state for East Asian and Pacific affairs under President George H.W. Bush and later president of the U.S. Institute of Peace. Swing recounted with a laugh, "He never went back to write his psychohistory of Mao."

Facing page: Early military and press fellows (clockwise from top left): Immanuel Klette (U.S. Air Force, 1965), Charles P. Tesh (U.S. Navy, 1969), Malcolm Browne (Murrow Fellow, 1966), and Sidney Berry (U.S. Army, 1967)

*Early International Affairs Fellowship
recipient Donald F. McHenry at a Council
event, 1982*

Decades later, Samantha Power, a Harvard University professor, was awarded a fellowship to study what more the United States could do to prevent genocide. Her book *"A Problem From Hell": America and the Age of Genocide* won the second annual Arthur Ross Book Award in 2003, and in 2005 the Council placed her as a fellow in the office of an Illinois senator who wanted to understand the range of policy options for ending violence in places such as Darfur. When that senator, Barack Obama, became president of the United States in 2009, he appointed Power to the National Security Council. In 2013, she became U.S. permanent representative to the United Nations.

The International Affairs Fellowship was not just an opportunity for academics to test their talent in the policy world. It was also offered to public servants who needed time away from their desks to study and research policy. Donald F. McHenry was stepping down as special assistant to the secretary of state when he was awarded the fellowship in 1971, and the Council secured for him a place as a guest scholar at the Brookings Institution, where he would study the role of American corporations in South Africa. He recalled:

> It was a period when there was a great pressure on campuses and among some of our nongovernmental organizations, trying to get American corporations to either disengage, disinvest, or what have you. At the same time, there was another movement which said, "Okay, you're there. While you're there in South Africa we want you to act responsibly and do what you can in terms of change." So that's what I did, I studied the engagement/disengagement debate.

McHenry traveled to South Africa to visit American factories. As he was a Black American with high-level ties in the State Department, the South African government took great pains to shore up its image and make sure McHenry was treated well. "But there were people outside of the South African government who weren't sure," McHenry recounted. "I remember going into a Ford Motor plant. Elaborate arrangements had been made for my arrival, and at the end of the day the director of the plant said to me, 'The Special Branch was here yesterday, and they said if anything happened to you there would be hell to pay. Who in the hell are you?'"

McHenry, who later rose through the ranks of the State Department, recalled taking part in meetings in the first week of Jimmy Carter's administration on the drafting of the so-called Sullivan Principles, which promoted corporate and social responsibility and put economic pressure on apartheid South Africa. "It was that two-year period of experience studying corporations that was very helpful in getting that movement going," he said. McHenry went on to serve as U.S. permanent representative to the United Nations under Carter and later became a member of the Council's Board of Directors.

Speaking on the fiftieth anniversary of the International Affairs Fellowship in 2017, CFR President Richard Haass called the program one of the most underappreciated things the Council does. Asked why, he replied,

> People often ask me what our business is, and I say, essentially, we don't produce doughnuts, we don't produce automobiles, but we produce ideas, and we're in the idea production and dissemination business, and we do it through the magazine, through meetings, through our scholars. We tend not to emphasize enough that we're also a talent developer in lots of ways, and this includes not just the international affairs fellows but also our investments in term members, military fellows, Studies fellows, as well as our research associates and interns.

Today, the International Affairs Fellowship program has over six hundred alumni.

VIETNAM AND FISSURES
IN THE ESTABLISHMENT

D espite the successful start of the Council's fellowship programs in the 1960s, a sense of unease pervaded Pratt House. The Vietnam War was turning the country upside down as anti-war protests and dissent grew. The foreign policy establishment was increasingly divided over whether and how to end the war. Tensions over Vietnam were initially muted at the Council, until a decision to rescind one fellowship offer created a major rupture between the staff and the Board of Directors.

In 1966, staff in CFR's Studies Program recommended Hans Morgenthau for a senior fellowship. Morgenthau had fled Nazi Germany to become an academic star in the United States. His work modernized the study of international relations and gave birth to the school of classical realism, with his *Politics Among Nations* serving as the textbook for a generation of scholars and practitioners. Morgenthau also happened to be one of the fiercest opponents of the Vietnam War and had been dismissed the previous year as an advisor to the Johnson administration because of his public dissent.

The old guard on the Council Board bristled. Frank Altschul and John J. McCloy were firm believers in the domino theory and held fast to the belief that the United States must prevail in Vietnam lest other countries fall under Soviet influence. McCloy was an unrelenting hawk unwilling to make any sacrifice on national security. Well before the Vietnam War, he was heavily involved in the government's decision to forcibly remove Japanese Americans from their homes on the West Coast to inland internment camps. He saw Morgenthau as a "radical upstart" whose appointment would destroy the Council. Altschul argued that the Council should take the unprecedented step of withdrawing its offer to Morgenthau, while McCloy and Armstrong

A crowd at a National Mobilization Committee to End the War in Vietnam direct action demonstration, Washington, DC, 1967

asserted that Morgenthau's fellowship would threaten the Council's access to the U.S. government.

Council staff and fellows rallied to Morgenthau's defense. John Temple Swing, George Franklin, Council Vice President David W. MacEachron, and Senior Fellows William J. Diebold and John C. Campbell "let it be known that if the Board refused to appoint Hans Morgenthau, the entire staff would resign en masse," according to Swing. The Board gave in, and Morgenthau became a visiting fellow in 1966. His fellowship gave him the opportunity to write *A New Foreign Policy for the United States.* The book came out in 1969 as a powerful critique of the Johnson administration's foreign policy, one that Stanley Hoffman, a Harvard professor and foreign policy expert, praised as "an important contribution to the current 'great debate' on America's role in the world. . . . I know of no more profound analysis of our Vietnam disaster than the twenty-seven pages Morgenthau devotes to the subject."

Toward the close of the decade, the United States was a country on edge. Public opinion had turned against the war by 1967, and the

Scholar Hans Morgenthau, whose appointment in 1966 caused controversy at CFR

Tet Offensive in 1968 further stunned the American public as Viet Cong and North Vietnamese forces engaged in sustained attacks to foment rebellion in South Vietnam and maximize American troop deaths. On April 4, 1968, just days after Johnson decided not to seek reelection, Martin Luther King Jr. was assassinated. Protests and riots raged across the country, and sit-ins paralyzed universities, including Columbia, where Grayson Kirk was president. A country that had in recent memory projected the image of a confident superpower seemed divided and weakened.

The Council avoided the subject of the war at the behest of McCloy, Altschul, and others on the Board. At one of a few meetings on Vietnam, McCloy glibly remarked to a reporter, "Well, certainly we had all the Bunkers and Lodges and the generals up explaining it." But study groups, which normally would have intensively studied any conflict involving so much American blood and treasure, bypassed serious discussion of the war or folded Vietnam into broader topics such as "Vietnam's Post-Conflict Prospects" (1967) and "United States Policy in South East and East Asia in the 1970s"

The office of Grayson Kirk at Columbia University during a student occupation, 1968

(1970–71). During the height of national divisions in 1968, the best the Council could do was arrange a study group aimlessly entitled "Ad Hoc Discussion on Vietnam," which was canceled after a few unsuccessful sessions.

CFR Vice President David MacEachron admitted that this avoidance had been a mistake but justified it, saying,

> The Council generally feels it is not in a good position to offer useful thoughts on a situation as rapidly moving as Vietnam and requiring operational decisions. Moreover, the CIA, the State Department, the Defense Department and the White House were knocking their brains out on it. We weren't sure what we could add.

By contrast, *Foreign Affairs* dissected the war in numerous articles, most notably Hamilton Armstrong's 1968 piece "Power in a Sieve" and Clark M. Clifford's 1969 article "A Viet Nam Reappraisal." Armstrong argued that no possible outcome in Vietnam could correspond

U.S. soldiers in Vietnam, 1967

with an American idea of victory. Clifford, President Johnson's secretary of defense, had resigned weeks earlier from the Pentagon, and his article argued that the United States needed to make an expeditious withdrawal of combat forces and give the fight over to the South Vietnamese while providing air cover. "The forces we now have deployed and the human and material costs we are now incurring have become, in my opinion, out of all proportion to our purpose. At current casualty rates, 10,000 more American boys will have lost their lives." Clifford concluded, "Let us start to bring our men home—and let us start now."

The magazine also published politicians, including Nelson A. Rockefeller, who wrote in his capacity as governor of New York and a progressive Republican running in the presidential primary in 1968, "A democracy cannot afford 'drop-outs' from the process of government. We must develop fresh premises that will demonstrate how our ideals remain relevant to the realities that confront the citizen. In the midst of perplexing technical problems, our deepest challenge is increasingly philosophical." Rather than comment on the nation's racial and civil rights woes, Rockefeller chose to focus on anti-war, anti-capitalist unrest at universities, sympathetically portraying students as disappointed idealists. Policymakers would have to develop fresh premises; otherwise, cynicism would deepen, and the public could "fall prey to demagogic appeals."

Rockefeller ultimately could not compete with Nixon, who remained a front-runner for much of the year. Nixon fended off bigger challenges from Michigan Governor George Romney and California Governor Ronald Reagan. Nixon, who had resigned his Council membership before running for office, published an article in *Foreign Affairs*, "Asia After Viet Nam," arguing that the United

States should acknowledge its status as a Pacific power and build a strong foreign policy to further its interests across Asia and go beyond a narrow, all-consuming focus on Vietnam. It was an early signal of how he would bring the United States out of the war and embrace the reality of China. "Taking the long view, we simply cannot afford to leave China forever outside the family of nations, there to nurture its fantasies, cherish its hates and threaten its neighbors. There is no place on this small planet for a billion of its potentially most able people to live in angry isolation."

Nixon's nomination win and Reagan's strong showing were a sign that the more progressive wings of the Republican party had atrophied. Although Nixon did not run against the northeastern establishment, his victory reflected that political power in the United States was moving south and west to the Sunbelt states, whose populations and economies were growing faster than those of the Northeast. Nixon would remake America's foreign policy with Henry Kissinger as his national security advisor.

PART TWO

A COUNCIL AND A COUNTRY DIVIDED

1969–92

THE COUNCIL WELCOMES WOMEN

Helen Caruso had not slept all night, thinking about what she would say at the 1969 Council staff retreat on Long Island the following day. It was a sad dilemma for the researcher, who usually had a way with words. She had written excellent papers for the Council's Middle East study groups over several years, and senior fellows such as John Campbell relied on her work. Yet she was not allowed into Council meetings to hear her papers being discussed because she was a woman.

Women had not been included in Council membership at its founding or in the decades that followed. That struck many people as wrong. But even in the late 1960s, there were Council members, staff, and officers in favor of the status quo, including Armstrong, who published remarkable female authors in the pages of *Foreign Affairs* but did not want women fully integrated into the Council.

The Council was not alone. Plenty of prestigious institutions at the time did not admit women, from the Century Association and the New York Athletic Club to Columbia College and Harvard College, but exclusion from Council membership and meeting attendance as a guest or staff member was causing serious discontent. Judith Gustafson, a senior executive assistant who started working at the Council in the 1960s, recalls the bizarre acrobatics she had to perform in keeping with Council policies that did not allow women into member meetings:

> I don't know how I figured this out . . . but I knew that certainly from the operational point of view I was very well aware, if George Franklin was someplace in the building in a meeting and I got a call that the chairman of

the Board wanted to talk to him immediately, the process was: I would write a note, I would go down to the meeting room, look around for the steward, who was the events manager of the time, who was male, who would take the note in to George Franklin while I waited outside, and if the steward wasn't around I would look for a staff member, or if I couldn't find a staff member I could even get the janitor because he was male. That person would go inside, and I would wait outside. I mean, it was quite clear.

When Caruso stood up after a sleepless night to speak at the Council retreat, staff members such as Gustafson were rooting for her. As one person at the retreat recounted, Caruso spoke about "what it was like to be a young woman on the Council staff, and to be involved in substantive work in the Council, and because she was a woman not being allowed to participate. And from that day on, Armstrong withdrew his active opposition to the admission of women as members." But Armstrong had not been the only one standing in the way.

The Council had last considered admitting women in 1954, and the Board of Directors overwhelmingly recommended against it. But 1969 was an altogether different era, and the movement for women's equality had spread to many sectors of the workforce and parts of the country. It was a reflection that the Council had fallen behind the times, even if it was in step with many of its peer, elite institutions.

A Council committee had been working on the matter for months, and many members and directors of the Board believed the Council needed to open its doors to female members. But even with Armstrong not standing in the way, certain people, including Council Board Chair John McCloy, were happy with the status quo.

Rita Hauser, a lawyer appointed to the United Nations by the Nixon administration, was happy to shake him out of his complacency. A colleague had suggested Hauser consider joining the Council, and she called to learn it was open only to men. Later, she attended a dinner with McCloy and said, "John, I'm very interested in the Council, but I see that it's only available to males, and I think that violates the civil rights laws, and I think it violates New York law."

He looked at her and said, "Really? You think so?"

"Absolutely," Hauser bluffed.

A couple days later, he called and asked, "Do you have any research on that item we were discussing?"

Shirley Temple Black and Rita Hauser, who were to become two of the earliest female members of the Council

Hauser did not, but she bluffed again. "Absolutely I do."

She quickly researched the matter after the call and sent McCloy a memo outlining that, according to civil rights laws and the laws of New York State, it was not permissible for a nonprofit organization to discriminate on the basis of sex. She finished by hinting, "I think you will be embarrassed if there is such a litigation." A few months later, McCloy called Hauser to say that the matter was on the agenda for a Board vote.

In November 1969, every Board member over sixty-five voted to reject admitting women, while younger members all voted for women to be integrated. The item passed the vote, barely. The following year, eight women were approved for life membership, including Katherine Graham, the legendary president of the *Washington Post*; Julia Henderson, director of the Bureau of Technical Assistance Operations at the United Nations; and Miriam Camps, vice chair of the Planning Council at the State Department. Not long after, two women took places on the Council's Board of Directors: Elizabeth Drew, a correspondent for the *Atlantic Monthly*, and Martha Redfield Wallace, executive director of the Henry Luce Foundation.

Hauser joined in 1971 and later was elected to the Board, Caruso took part in study groups in which she discussed and defended her own work, and Gustafson no longer needed men to pass along notes for her and could attend Council meetings at her leisure.

THE CHANGING OF THE GUARD

The vote to admit women was just one of many transformational changes at the Council. In 1970, David Rockefeller replaced McCloy as chair. Rockefeller had been a member of the Council since 1941 and the youngest member to join the Board. Already a globally recognized name for his leadership at Chase Manhattan and his work as a billionaire philanthropist, Rockefeller wanted the Council to become more modern and broader. He saw the old guard as too restricted in their outlook:

> I would say very conservative. Ham Armstrong often differed from the mainstream in his views, but he and his close colleagues were interested in their own ideas, and people who thought as they did. I do not think they were interested in seeing the Council broaden out and include the rest of the world. They liked it as their own little club. . . . It seemed to me that if the Council was going to play the kind of role which I felt it should, it needed to broaden its membership beyond the rather narrow group of Wall Street bankers, financiers, lawyers, and smattering of academics . . . and add younger people, and over time I was one of those who supported including women. So I suppose I was viewed by some as a young person getting involved in things I did not know much about.

With the support of Rockefeller and forward-looking staff and Board members, a new category of membership was introduced, inviting promising individuals in their twenties and thirties to join the Council for a five-year term. Thus, the Term Member Program was

A group of term members, early 1970s

inaugurated to infuse the Council with younger voices from diverse fields who could bring fresher views and new perspectives on foreign policy. It was also a way to test people out for permanent or life membership in the Council without making any promises.

Going forward, the Council would also have a full-time president leading the way rather than rely on the spare time afforded to it by executives such as Grayson Kirk and Russell Leffingwell. In 1971, Rockefeller and Cyrus Vance, who had joined the Board in 1968 after resigning his post as deputy secretary of defense in the Johnson administration, recruited Bayless Manning, dean of the law school at Stanford University, to lead the Council.

Manning was not a foreign policy expert, but, as the Council's first full-time, salaried president, he revamped governance and shook up operations. He instituted new election procedures and term limits for the Board of Directors—some Board members had been in place since the Council's first years. Manning streamlined staff positions and constantly looked for ways to make things work better, whether planning for women's bathrooms or asking staff for recommendations

The Council's first full-time president, Bayless Manning

to improve the organization. If he was not in his office, he could often be found chatting with staff in the mail room.

Staff members either loved or disliked him, but none were indifferent to his management style. Gustafson, who worked as Manning's executive assistant, recalled, "He was thought of as pretty much a cold fish. He was extremely, frighteningly intelligent, and he worked extremely hard, and everybody else who was involved within his circle had to work pretty hard too." He was exactly what the Council needed at the time, although his ways made some bristle. "There was a Board meeting where he wanted to get everyone's attention, and they were not coming to order, and he whistled, this loud shrill whistle," Gustafson recounted.

Manning frustrated Armstrong, who was accustomed to telling the Council what ought to be done and how. For fifty years, Armstrong had filled the pages of *Foreign Affairs* while steering the Council's agendas in the Meetings and Studies Programs. The popularity of the magazine and Armstrong's power across the organization in those years were the tail that wagged the dog that was CFR.

At one point, Armstrong had asked Franklin D. Roosevelt to consider becoming Council president. He wrote copious letters to Indian Prime Minister Indira Gandhi for over a decade, asking her to take part in Council activities and write for the magazine; he demanded that Samuel Huntington, professor of government at Harvard University, write clearer and shorter pieces; and he banned Hans Morgenthau and Pulitzer Prize–winning journalist and political commentator Walter Lippmann from the pages of the magazine. While Armstrong disliked Morgenthau intellectually, he despised Lippmann for personal reasons. Lippmann had had an affair with and subsequently married Armstrong's wife, which could also explain why Armstrong, even after he withdrew opposition to women joining the Council, remained adamantly opposed to allowing the spouses of members to join in events.

Armstrong was incredulous that Manning would not take his advice on Council business, including for the fiftieth anniversaries of the Council and *Foreign Affairs*, which Armstrong thought should be high-profile, lavish affairs. But the Board was easing Armstrong into retirement, and Manning was eager to assert his management.

With Armstrong on the brink of retirement and Manning in charge of the Council, a new balance was starting to take shape: a church-state separation of sorts between the Council and the magazine that would grow over the years, solidifying the edito-

Alton Frye expanded the Council's programming efforts in Washington, DC.

rial independence of the magazine. The Council and the magazine were also becoming more realistic about their mission. *Foreign Affairs* reflected this evolution with a subtle change in its mission statement. It would no longer seek to "guide American public opinion" on foreign policy but "inform" it. Still, there were moments when leadership at the Council and *Foreign Affairs* were overconfident about the future. Writing on the eve of the fiftieth anniversary, Armstrong told the Board that a new journal called *Foreign Policy* "will not be competition worth worrying about." That prediction would not hold.

Other changes were coming around the time of the fiftieth anniversary. In 1971, the roster of programs expanded to include a fellowship for Senior Foreign Service officers. The Council opened a modest presence in Washington, DC, in a small rented space. The office was inaugurated with little fanfare to give Alton Frye, a former international affairs fellow, time to shape the work and figure out how to best support the Council's mission. The Washington office would grow slowly but steadily to serve membership in the capital and bring the Council's work closer to policymakers who worked in the White House, Capitol Hill, the State Department, and other federal agencies but did not have time to travel to New York for Council events.

One change that brought immediate repercussions was the selection of a new editor for *Foreign Affairs*. Before offering the Council presidency to Bayless Manning, Rockefeller had asked William Bundy if he was interested in the job. Bundy had been teaching at Harvard after stepping down as advisor to the Kennedy and Johnson administrations on the Vietnam War. Bundy had politely declined. Rockefeller then offered him the editorship of *Foreign Affairs* when the two met at Harvard for a football game. Rockefeller may have been an agent of change on behalf of diversity and modernization, yet he still did some things the old-school way.

The reaction was furious. Members who were opposed to the Vietnam War rose up in protest. How could Bundy, who, according to the *New York Times*, had his name "on more pieces of paper dealing with Vietnam over a seven-year period than anyone else," who at one point suggested heavily bombing North Vietnam to trigger a crisis and force the United Nations to negotiate a settlement, who was called foul names by anti-war protesters, possibly be the right person to impartially and objectively fill the pages of *Foreign Affairs*?

Letters poured in as Bundy's nomination became public. Angry members wrote to Rockefeller, as did those who supported Bundy. Richard H. Ullman, a Princeton professor who later became the Council's director of Studies, wrote to protest the appointment. (He later regretted his opposition and grew to like Bundy.) George H.W. Bush, at the time the chief of the U.S. Liaison Office in China and de facto U.S. ambassador to the country, sent a postcard expressing his enthusiasm for Bundy. Even members who happened to be writing to the Council about other matters were compelled to say something; in a letter announcing that he was resigning his membership, George Kennan was careful to point out that the reasons were solely due to his professional obligations. Rockefeller spent many hours writing tailored responses and scrambled to control the damage to Manning, who had barely settled into his new office. But before the Bundy controversy cooled, another crisis hit.

In October 1971, the Council surrendered to the FBI a paper that Daniel Ellsberg had authored months earlier for a study group. Ellsberg was a former Pentagon employee who had given a classified study on Vietnam (later known as the Pentagon Papers) to the press. The Council's response to the FBI subpoena brought swift condemnation from a host of members, most notably from Supreme Court Justice Arthur J. Goldberg, who was "shocked and surprised" by the Council's decision and asked for a special meeting "to repair the abridgement of free speech, association and expressions which has occurred." Ellsberg chimed in, telling the press, "I was very disheartened at one more demonstration of a group of people who have forgotten or put to sleep their own sense of constitutional rights."

The controversy over the Ellsberg paper was not about the content. Bundy and others who had read the paper determined that it had nothing to do with the leaked Pentagon study; rather, the issue was one of confidentiality and confidence: confidentiality of the Council's proceedings as a members-only organization and confidence in its capacity to uphold its standards. But Manning was a lawyer at heart and weighed things differently. "He had great respect for the law, and his point was that, despite the value of the Council's tradition, the court order was a court order, and you simply could not ignore it," Gustafson said.

The Vietnam War unleashed anguish and passions that were not easy to keep in check. Joseph Nye Jr., a CFR member and professor of international affairs at Harvard University, recalls many turbulent episodes: his office at the Center for International Affairs was ransacked because it used to be Henry Kissinger's, and, during a 1971 meeting that McCloy was attending, protestors forced their way in past the police. "I can remember one of these protestors picking up a pitcher of water and pouring it on McCloy, and I thought, boy, that could not happen at the Council," Nye said.

Vietnam bitterly divided the Board and membership for years, and the chasm deepened as new members came into the Council. Richard K. Betts, professor of security studies at Columbia University, explained, "Members of the Council would not have called themselves neo-isolationists, but a lot of them were in favor of retrenchment. A lot of them voted for George McGovern, and he wanted to cut the Defense budget by a third." In the 1970s, Betts was a fellow in the Council's Washington office and worked with Leslie H. Gelb, then a correspondent and senior fellow at Brookings, on a book entitled *The Irony of Vietnam: The System Worked*. Betts noted the title was giving people heartburn decades later: "The idea that you can say anything worked in connection with the Vietnam War understandably drives people nuts. Our argument was that the policy was a disaster, but the process by which it developed worked pretty much as people expect it to in a democracy. Some people could accept that and gag on the implications, and others still didn't."

THE COUNCIL ADRIFT

T he Council's fiftieth anniversary dinner took place on September 28, 1972, an unusual choice, as the organization had been founded July 29, 1921. But the date mattered far less than the mood, which was not entirely joyous. McCloy delivered a speech filled with caustic remarks about a growing tendency in the press and public opinion to disparage the establishment. He rattled off names of many of those seated in the room and declared:

> People distinguished in the government, education, business, and professional life of the country. Call them "elite" if you will. I do not seem to shrink back at that word as readily as would some. I would hope that the Council will always be able to draw from its own ranks on the capacities and the experience of members of uncommon quality. . . . We have been operating for a period of fifty years, accomplishing, I venture to say, in very full measure the fundamental objectives the founders had in mind; namely to extend significantly the content and quality of our thinking in regard to international affairs. We also have had a creditable record among our membership in direct service to the government in war and peace. It is a record, I believe, at which only a definite malcontent could cavil.

In referencing malcontents, McCloy might have been thinking of John Kenneth Galbraith, who had resigned his membership in a highly public way the previous year, citing boredom and telling a journalist, "Most of the proceedings involve a level of banality so deep that the only question they raise is whether one should sit through them," or possibly of J. Anthony Lukas, who had published a long article in the *New York Times* blasting the Council as a has-been establishment, short on good ideas. Although Lukas's piece was unbalanced and mean-spirited overall, his conclusion rang true:

> The Council as an institution cannot expect to play the central role it often has in the past: because of animosity toward the New York elite from high in the Nixon Administration; because new centers of influence—Los Angeles, Dallas, Atlanta—have sprung up; because the government's own foreign-policy expertise has vastly expanded; because university departments of international relations and independent centers like the Brookings Institution have mushroomed; and because, in the wake of Vietnam, the public's tolerance for a self-elected, self-perpetuating foreign-policy elite is rapidly diminishing.

It was, by most standards, not a successful anniversary year. *Foreign Affairs* was facing growing competition from *Foreign Policy* magazine, which Samuel Huntington had cofounded in 1970 as a fresher, more contemporary venue for readers and writers. Circulation at *Foreign Affairs* was stagnant, hovering in the low to mid-seventy thousands, a noticeable drop from the record of eighty thousand set in 1968. As editor, Bundy would receive mixed reviews. For every piece that resonated with readers and brought plaudits, many more fell flat and ran far too long. Bundy was the worst offender, publishing his own articles that were two to three times the length of those he published by George Kennan or Arthur Schlesinger. More than a few members and subscribers were irked enough to write letters of complaint throughout the decade. "Why does *Foreign Affairs* have to be so sober?" wrote one member while grumbling about the length and jargon.

Changes were easier to advocate than to implement, and even earnest initiatives often raised expectations beyond the Council leadership's ability to meet them. On September 20, 1972, a week before the anniversary dinner, David Rockefeller received a letter from a new initiative called the Women's Rights Project at the American Civil Liberties Union. The writer of the letter, a lawyer by the name of Ruth Bader Ginsburg, was eager to understand what the Council was doing to fully integrate women. Manning's office responded that November with a sufficiently vague and institutional letter assuring Ginsburg that "appropriate measures" were being taken.

Ruth Bader Ginsburg would become a Council member in 1974.

Yet, the integration of women was tougher in membership than it was in staff positions and fellowship appointments. Two years after the decision to admit women, the Council counted 28 women among 1,551 members (1.8 percent of the total). Five years later, that number had risen to 70 of 1,725 (4 percent of the total). The numbers would inch upward slowly, especially as the Council at the time sought modest increases in its total number of members. This did not deter Ginsburg, who entered the Council's membership roster in 1974, which was the year before International Women's Year, marked by the first global conference on women in Mexico City.

At *Foreign Affairs*, Bundy was happy to report that many positions had been filled by women: "Our contributions to International Women's Year are already substantial: Doris Forest and Grace Darling in charge of our business affairs and promotion. Elizabeth Bryant handling the books, and Barbara Schwarz and Evelyn Morel assisting the editors in ways beyond count. And Jennifer Whitaker has stirred up the Mexico City gathering for our only remaining need—more women as authors!" Whitaker herself had written a riveting article that October, "Women of the World: A Report From Mexico City," which laid out "a microcosm of the differences which confront the women's movement as it gains international legitimacy," particularly the huge differences between the feminist movement in the West and women's movements in poor countries.

In 1973, on the eve of the global oil crisis, the Council seemed adrift. It still had the convening power to put together high-profile meetings and bring world leaders to speak, and it retained an exceptionally accomplished membership. For example, David Rockefeller convened a group of private citizens from North America, Western Europe, and Japan to foster closer cooperation, particularly in the economic sphere. The core group included Council members Zbigniew Brzezinski, George Franklin, and Paul Volcker, Nixon's undersecretary of the treasury for international affairs. The meeting gave birth to the Trilateral Commission, a forward-looking body that viewed growing economic interdependence as a fact that should be harnessed in service of global prosperity rather than be treated as a problem to be rolled back. If the Council had not existed as a space for people like Brzezinski to build networks, it is difficult to know whether an equivalent body would exist today.

But on the whole, the Council's energy and creativity were depleted, and the classic study groups that had been its mainstay and launched the careers of members such as Henry Kissinger were no longer going strong. To address this, Manning and Ullman decided to launch the 1980s Project, which sought to anticipate the foreign policy issues of the near future and develop ways for policymakers to rise to the challenges. Study groups produced nearly two dozen books and many papers on less conventional topics—disaster relief, global human rights, and international political economy.

The problem with the 1980s Project was that some at the Council perceived it as "bureaucratic, lumbering, and not particularly dynamic," in the words of soon-to-be CFR President Winston Lord. Nye gave Manning credit for spurring people to think about the future but said that ultimately "his bad luck was that events changed the focus of attention away from many of the things that were involved in the project as we structured it. Which reminds one of the Harold Macmillan response to somebody who said, 'What are the major problems that you face as a political leader?' And he said, 'Events, dear boy, events.'" The 1980s Project could not have foreseen the Soviet invasion of Afghanistan, the surprise election of Ronald Reagan, or the breakdown of détente.

Nor did Manning expect that funding from Ford and other foundations, which had enabled the Council to run so many projects, would dry up in the economic scarcity of the mid-1970s. By 1977, Manning figured that he had sufficiently updated the Council. During a conversation with David Rockefeller, he mused casually about stepping down. Rockefeller mistook his ambivalence for determination, telling the Board, "Well, Bayless Manning is leaving now, and we have to start thinking about a new president of the Council." With that, Manning unceremoniously departed.

AN UNCERTAIN COURSE

n 1977, the changes kept coming. Jimmy Carter was inaugurated president of the United States after defeating Gerald R. Ford, Apple was incorporated, *Star Wars* opened in cinemas, the Concorde started flying between London and New York, record blizzards pummeled the Midwest, deadly heat waves fried Europe, the last case of smallpox was detected in Somalia, Spain brought decades of Francoist rule to an end with its first democratic elections, Zia-ul-Haq overthrew the elected government in Pakistan, Anwar al-Sadat became the first Arab leader to formally visit Israel, Deng Xiaoping was rehabilitated and took the reins of the Chinese Communist Party, the U.S. Department of Energy was created to cope with recurring oil crises, and the Sex Pistols' debut punk album rose to the top of charts usually crowned with safer pop artists.

Nothing could be taken for granted anymore in a fast-changing world, including the predominance of the United States and the Council. But the Council's new president, Winston Lord, was an optimist who thought the United States still had plenty of room to maneuver and commanded plenty of respect. "Although we're no longer the dominant, neither are we pawns of destiny," he remarked. Lord understood both the need for change and the importance of trying new strategies. In 1971, he had traveled with Kissinger and Nixon to negotiate a delicate rapprochement with Beijing. Later, as head of policy planning in the Ford administration, he argued that an emerging emphasis on human rights could be merged with realpolitik in foreign policy and convinced Kissinger to place more emphasis on cultural values and norms in his speeches during visits to Africa's newly independent states.

Cars in line for gas, 1979

Lord's hopeful tone boosted morale at the Council, during a time when many experts were arguing that America was in decline. Yet Lord did not downplay the challenges ahead. "The Council on Foreign Relations is in trouble," he told the Board of Directors. "In some cases we are drawing down our capital and living off our past reputation." While Manning had modernized the Council's internal workings and brought in female members, Lord worried that the organization was still falling behind the times, losing touch with the world outside its walls. As he put it,

> For a good part of its history, the Council was the dom-
> inant think tank, the dominant foreign policy institution
> in America, particularly in the Cold War period, when
> it was even working closely with the government. It was
> Eurocentric, as was our foreign policy, looking across
> the Atlantic. The overwhelming membership was along
> the East Coast, particularly in New York City, and it was
> overwhelmingly white and male. Now, that had begun to
> change in the sixties and seventies, but we were still fac-
> ing a catch-up situation.

CFR President Winston Lord with former U.S. President Jimmy Carter, 1983

Lord aimed to strengthen the Council with a strategy. Indeed, it was the first time the organization had an overarching strategy in a modern, corporate sense. His goals included bolstering the Studies Program, extending the Council's reach beyond New York, and securing the Council's finances. The Studies Program was understaffed and overworked. He explained, "I was dismayed to discover that of a total staff of about ninety-five, there were only four full-time senior study people." Library staff, who provided critical research support, had been cut back, and Studies was so beleaguered that the director John Campbell postponed his retirement to continue what Lord considered a "superhuman" job.

As far as the Council's ability to reach more people nationally, Lord thought that membership was too centered on New York. Of the Council's 1,778 members, 743 were in New York, 348 in Washington, DC, and 110 in Boston. The remaining 577 were scattered across the rest of the country, especially in the Great Lakes region and California. Lord rhetorically asked the Board, "How meaningful is membership for someone who only gets *Foreign Affairs* and may catch an occasional meeting in New York when his schedule permits but doesn't really have a feel for what the Council is up to?" Financially, the Council was running deficits and had made cuts to staff and programs, and many Studies initiatives were being carried out on an ad hoc basis. Lord warned that it would take at least two years to address the most basic problems.

Still, the Council had its share of successes. It remained a source for talent that the government occasionally tapped. When Carter restructured his administration in July 1977, he selected three Council directors for vital posts: Paul Volcker as chair of the Federal Reserve Board, Hedley Donovan as senior advisor on domestic and foreign policy and media relations, and Lloyd Cutler as counsel to the president. Carter himself would be the guest of honor at a December 1981 "Meeting for Members and Their Spouses"—events such as this episodically opened the Council to family and friends of members to showcase the benefits of belonging.

The Meetings Program continued to have strong convening power. In 1979, it hosted Moshe Dayan, Israel's minister of foreign affairs, and in 1981 Egypt's President Anwar al-Sadat. David Rockefeller had the honor of showing Sadat around Pratt House, and Sadat spoke on the challenges and hopes he saw in normalizing relations with Israel. Months after his visit, Sadat was assassinated in Cairo.

The Council's work on Africa was one surprising area of strength, despite overall financial and staff constraints. Study groups examined military factors in African politics, and fellows produced a series of works, including Crawford Young's "Ideology, Politics, and Development Choice in Africa" and William Zartman's "Ripe for Resolution: Crises and Intervention in African Conflicts."

Meetings featured an array of African political figures. In 1979, the Council hosted Zaire's President Mobutu Sese Seko and President of the National Union for the Total Independence of Angola Jonas Savimbi, who spoke about Angola's future in the wake of its independence from Portugal. Also on the roster in 1979 was Helen Suzman, member of parliament from South Africa and anti-apartheid advocate, who spoke about the prospects for change. The end of apartheid was more than a decade away, yet Suzman did not shy away from challenging the country's establishment. Mark Suzman, CFR member and CEO of the Bill and Melinda Gates Foundation, fondly recalled his aunt's fearlessness: she once told Prime Minister John Vorster, who ruled South Africa when Nelson Mandela was sentenced to life imprisonment, that Vorster and his political allies should go see a segregated township for themselves but first

"heavily disguise themselves as human beings."

Lord's toughest challenge as president came by way of the Board election in the summer of 1981. Since Manning's scrupulous governance reforms, the Board election process had been altered a number of times, creating a complicated, quirky system. Incumbents could run for their slots, but for any vacancy two candidates would be added to the ballot. The formula led to an unusual situation in June when for eight slots on the Board there were seven incumbents, so that nine members were competing for eight total spots. Kissinger was among those up for reelection. A disaster was in the making. Looking back on the election, Lord said:

President of Zaire Mobutu Sese Seko

Just figure it out. If you're going to drop one person when you're voting, the person who's the most controversial and the best known is going to be in deep trouble. And obviously, in the wake of Vietnam and many other issues Henry was controversial. Even though people now forget, during the Ford administration, Henry was the single most admired person and respected not only abroad but in the United States—man of the year, superman, held this country together in the wake of Watergate—in my opinion, was extremely powerful. Nevertheless, because of Vietnam, and détente with respect to the right wing, he was controversial.

Facing page: Egyptian President Anwar al-Sadat and CFR Chair David Rockefeller at the Harold Pratt House, 1981

83

As the votes were coming in, Lord could see that Kissinger was losing even with three-fourths of members voting for him. Gustafson said, "Things were just in chaos here . . . and Winston was just beside himself." At the conclusion of the election, Lord reported the distressing results and called Kissinger to express his regret. "It was the worst day of my professional life," Lord said. The incident greatly complicated Kissinger's relationship with the Council and its membership over the years.

Despite the massive changes in foreign policy, Kissinger's election loss was a sign that the country—including members of the foreign policy establishment—was not ready to give up the ghost of Vietnam. The Vietnam legacy made itself felt as late as 1995, when Robert McNamara came to present his memoir, *In Retrospect*. McNamara had been one of the architects of the Vietnam War and served as secretary of defense during the Kennedy and Johnson administrations. At the Council event, Hauser sat in the audience with Bundy, Rockefeller, and Kissinger. After McNamara's talk and one or two polite questions, Hauser recalled that a member of the audience stood and said, "I was an admiral in the navy. My father was an admiral. My grandfather was an admiral, my great-grandfather was an admiral, and we had a long tradition of service, and I resigned because of you, because of what you did, because of how you lied, and how you didn't live up to your duties as secretary of defense." Hauser said, "The place went quiet as a tomb," and McNamara was visibly shaken for the rest of the meeting.

On February 8, 1983, Lord presented the Board of Directors with a memo entitled "The Future of the Council." The memo outlined the Council's successes: The Council had preserved its core Studies work on the Soviet Union, military strategy, economic issues, and Western Europe. Members were becoming more involved, and attendance at Council events was up 60 percent over previous years. The Council's first television show, produced by WNET, featured Marilyn Berger as moderator while Council members threw questions at a panel of foreign policy experts.

But the Council's past glories felt remote, and Lord saw the need for greater changes to the Studies Program, Meetings Program, and National Program. Studies still required major investments; the program had four permanently funded fellows when it needed eight, especially to cover Asia, Latin America, the Middle East, and science and technology. The Council, explained Lord, was facing growing competition from other institutions:

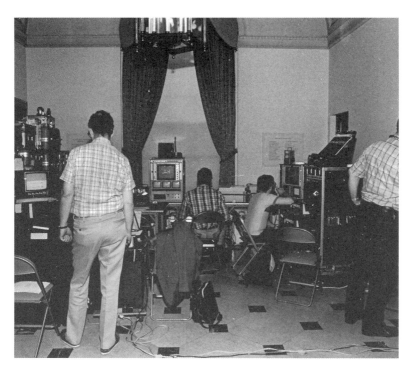

Production crew from WNET during a taping of an episode of the Council's first television program

> The arena in which we operate is not that of ten years ago or even five. Many more institutions now offer forums to foreign policy experts. In New York, for example, the [Foreign Policy Association] is actively trying to energize its program and successfully competed with us for major visitors such as Margaret Thatcher, Indira Gandhi, Zia-ul-Haq, and Hosni Mubarak.

Meetings were expensive, and the Council was forgoing opportunities to host more world leaders because of a lack of money.

Expanding the Council's national reach had been, in Lord's words, "possibly the most difficult goal." Soon after Lord became president, he had made an effort to bring in more members from regions in the United States that were underrepresented in membership, particularly the West Coast, Midwest, and South. Although there were now thirty-seven Committees on Foreign Relations, they had not served the Council well in identifying suitable members outside the East Coast. The

Maurice R. Greenberg and Cyrus Vance, both of whom would serve as vice chair of CFR's Board of Directors

quality of the committees was uneven, and maintaining relations with them took time and effort. Lord saw national reach as a way to bring more people from other parts of the country into CFR membership and to take the Council to them. This was done through large conferences the Council held in cities such as San Francisco, Denver, Houston, and Minneapolis and through biannual trips for members to military bases at home and abroad, where they could learn about strategic defense issues with members of the military. The conferences and trips allowed Council members from New York and Washington, DC, to mix with members from other parts of the country.

But sustaining the work required money, and Lord announced the Campaign for the Council to raise $14.5 million, a vast sum in those days. Fortunately, Rockefeller liked Lord's vision, and the two worked to win over Board members one by one, starting with Walter Wriston, chief executive of Citibank. On a December day in 1984, after just forty-five minutes with Maurice R. Greenberg, CFR member and chair of American International Group, Lord and Wriston secured $1.5 million to support a fellow for Asia. Rockefeller wrote to Greenberg, thanking him for his "wonderful munificence"—initially Greenberg had pledged just $1,000.

Lord did much to expand giving to the Council. During his presidency, the number of members donating beyond their annual dues grew from 160 to 1,000 (approximately half of membership). He expanded the Corporation Service Program, which had been formed back in 1953 to bring to the Council more business executives who wanted insights into major political and economic problems that could affect business. At its inception, the twenty-five firms that subscribed to the Corporate Program included the Arabian American Oil Company (today

Early members of the Corporate Program included Singer and Pan Am.

Saudi Aramco), Brown Brothers Harriman, Chase National Bank (today JPMorgan Chase), General Motors Overseas Operations, IBM World Trade Corporation, Pan American World Airways, and the RAND Corporation. Altogether, the subscription fees brought in $38,517 that first year. Lord brought in new companies and expanded the activities of the program, and by the end of his tenure the Corporate Program was adding $1 million a year to the Council's budget (20 percent of the total).

Despite the financial successes and the expansion of Council activities, Lord faced a number of challenges. The nationwide Committees on Foreign Relations continued to multiply. Some, such as the Honolulu committee, were robust, while others were fragile or prone to escalating their troubles to the Council. A member of the Santa Barbara committee wrote to complain about the committee's policy of excluding spouses, explaining that the rule prohibited him from bringing his wife to meetings but technically allowed anyone who wished to bring a mistress. Lord responded frequently to these letters, but his hands were tied. The committees were largely autonomous from the Council and free to do as they pleased. It was not clear that the relationship was worth the effort the Council was putting into them. A fight was brewing.

CHANGED LEADERSHIP
IN RESTLESS TIMES

The year was 1985. Détente with the Soviet Union had faded as Ronald Reagan was sworn in for a second term. Christa McAuliffe was selected to be the first teacher in space, and musicians took part in Live Aid, a major concert that raised money for famine relief in Ethiopia. It was a year of airplane and cruise ship hijackings and terror attacks at the Rome and Vienna airports. CEOs and politicians were taking huge risks, from the disastrous introduction of New Coke to the start of an arms race with the Soviet Union. It was also the year that Gorbachev became general secretary of the Soviet Communist Party.

At *Foreign Affairs*, Bundy was stepping down. He had been a principled editor and even turned down an article on Latin America by David Rockefeller. He had opened up the pages of *Foreign Affairs* to fierce criticism of his own views of Vietnam and gone to great lengths to court world leaders, including Fidel Castro, to contribute articles. In a letter to the Cuban leader, Bundy referenced other leaders published in *Foreign Affairs*—India's Jawaharlal Nehru, West Germany's Willy Brandt, and the Soviet Union's Nikita Khrushchev. Bundy made the case that U.S.-Cuba relations deserved more thoughtful analysis and pointed out that the magazine would pay $750 for Castro's submission. Castro never wrote that article, but he would later visit the Council and invite members to visit Havana.

The magazine had not fully shaken off the stodginess and dense writing that characterized it in the mid-1970s. Circulation temporarily spiked in 1981, reaching one hundred thousand for the first time in the magazine's history, before falling again. By 1985, the magazine was struggling to reach ninety thousand.

President Ronald Reagan in the Oval Office, 1985

The search for an editor was narrowed down to a few names. When Leslie H. Gelb dropped out, William G. Hyland, an expert on Soviet affairs who had served in the Nixon administration with Kissinger, became the front-runner. Hyland said, "After I got the [*Foreign Affairs*] job, of course, Nixon being Nixon, he immediately called me and said, 'It's a terrible place, but I'm glad you are doing it.'" Nixon had resigned his Council membership in the 1960s, and, unlike Kennan who had come back to the Council after a hiatus, Nixon had not been invited to reinstate his membership. He had not paid his dues, and his scorn for the Council was documented in his conversations with staff on the Nixon White House tapes: "I'm going to get that Council on Foreign Relations. I'm going to chop those bastards off right at the neck."

Hyland and his managing editor, Peter Grose, aimed to modernize the magazine, making it more accessible in its prose and more topical. Some of the first articles included Walter Laquer's "Reflections on Terrorism," Louis Henkin's "Foreign Affairs and the Constitution," and George Kennan's "Containment, Then and Now" on the fortieth anniversary of his X article. When Hyland ran into Nixon after a few issues had been published, the former president took another jab: "You're a good editor. The magazine's very good. Of course, no one reads it."

Hyland was kind, thoughtful, and witty, but he had no tolerance for vapid statements by politicians and diplomats. After he turned down an article by the Dutch prime minister, the embassy of the Netherlands threatened to lodge a formal protest. Hyland replied, "Mr. Ambassador, we're not the State Department." He declined to publish Patrick Moynihan's article on the CIA that he thought was mean-spirited. He told Moynihan, "You may be a prestigious senator from

Incoming Foreign Affairs *Editor William G. Hyland (right) meeting with Editor William Bundy, 1984*

New York, but that doesn't mean that you're entitled to write articles." And he ruffled a few feathers when he published Nixon's article on summitry ahead of Reagan's arms control meeting with Gorbachev. One reporter called him and said, "The rehabilitation of Nixon owes a lot to you and that article." Hyland replied, "Well, I wanted to have an article about summitry, and I thought Nixon would be a good author, and he would get a lot of attention."

Major leadership changes were in play at the Council as well. David Rockefeller handed the chairmanship over to Peter G. Peterson, a former Republican secretary of commerce who had become a successful investment banker. And Lord accepted President Reagan's offer to serve as U.S. ambassador to China, leaving the Council in need of a new president. A search committee reviewed the qualifications of more than seventy-five men and women and decided to offer the Council presidency to Peter Tarnoff, a distinguished career diplomat who was serving as executive director of the World Affairs Council in San Francisco.

Fanfare over Tarnoff's appointment was overshadowed when word leaked that some officers of the Board had favored another candidate. Brent Scowcroft, national security advisor to President Ford and member of the Council's Board, had backed Robert C. McFarlane, who had stepped down as Reagan's national security advisor earlier that December. Cyrus Vance had strongly endorsed Tarnoff. Rumors circulated for days in the press that Kissinger and Scowcroft were concerned that "elite liberalism" had tainted the Council and that they had launched a "vociferous campaign" against Tarnoff's candidacy. Scowcroft would have to wait until 2003 for his next candidate to become the Council's president.

In focusing on the squabbles over the presidency, the press exaggerated partisan divides at the Council. There were other differences to consider between the two front-runners: McFarlane wanted to redouble the Council's work in Washington, DC, and focus more on the policy establishment. Tarnoff wanted the Council to expand its work to other parts of the country and make it more national in its outlook. The Board chose the latter.

Tarnoff faced a dilemma at the outset. The Council needed to build its endowment to support new initiatives and sustain the fellows. Only one of the Council's nine study areas was fully endowed, the Washington office had scant staff, and membership was far from representing most of the country (New Yorkers made up 42 percent of the Council's approximately 2,500 members in 1987). Members were restive and worried. Cyrus Vance, vice chair of the Council, suggested that Tarnoff commission a survey of members. The survey revealed concerns that the Council was not playing enough of a role in American foreign policy, and members feared the organization would become irrelevant.

The Council continued to have episodic impact, and its work was serious enough to occasionally upset government officials. A senior member of the Reagan administration accosted Tarnoff near the White House after Alton Frye wrote an article that criticized Reagan's policies. "You've got to do something about Frye," the official demanded. "He's beating up on the president."

Tarnoff replied, "What do you mean? This one lone guy at the Council is beating up on the president of the United States? You're telling me that he's doing harm to Ronald Reagan and that Ronald Reagan can't take care of himself?"

But the Council activity that would have the most impact in this period would take place not in New York or Washington but in Moscow.

MOSCOW ON THE HUDSON

t was a stunning trip, full of revelations and a sign that the
Council was still relevant. In February 1987, a Council delegation consisting of Tarnoff, Peterson, Kissinger, Hyland, Vance,
and Jeane J. Kirkpatrick, who had been the U.S. permanent
representative to the United Nations in the Reagan administration,
visited the Soviet Union and held detailed discussions with Mikhail
Gorbachev and dissidents such as Andrei Sakharov. Gorbachev had
been running the Soviet Union for only two years, and U.S. leaders
had doubts about his intentions and sincerity. Gorbachev started
the meeting by attacking Kissinger and Kirkpatrick for their policies
toward the Soviet Union. Peterson had spent time in Moscow during
his government service and understood the issues at stake. He looked
at Gorbachev as he tried to defuse the tension:

> Mr. General Secretary, we're happy to be with you, and we
> can continue this kind of discussion indefinitely if you like,
> but I wonder to what end. I would have thought that we
> both have a common interest here [in] the field where I've
> spent much of my life, the international economic field. It
> occurs to me that both you and we are facing some very
> formidable competition in terms of technology know-
> how, and that the more we spend so much of our precious
> resources in an adversarial relationship with each other,
> the less likely we are twenty and thirty years from now to
> be able to look back to our children and grandchildren and
> say, "We really invested our resources very productively."

Gorbachev replied, "Well, now, that's a question worth talking about."

Former Soviet Premier Mikhail Gorbachev meeting with Peter G. Peterson and Henry Kissinger in Moscow, 1987

The mood lightened, and a three-hour discussion followed. Gorbachev impressed the group with his sincerity in pushing ahead with perestroika, restructuring and reforming the Soviet system. Tarnoff recalls Gorbachev saying:

> Look, I am fifty-two. If I only had ten years to live, I could probably continue this system. I could probably continue to do things as we've been doing in the past. But I come from a long-living, healthy family. I'm going to live another twenty-five years, and this system is unsustainable for that period of time. . . . And I'm going to change it politically. I'm going to open up the system so there can be less corruption, more criticism, within the confines of our state.

Back at the Council, members of the delegation held a meeting to report their impressions. Vance told the assembled members and officers that it was time to reject the attitude that "whatever helps them is bad for us." Kissinger was the most cautious, admitting that he was impressed by Gorbachev but that there were many unknowns. In his report, he noted:

> We have to remember that when we discuss reform we are speaking at this moment of a theory, and not yet of a practice. It has just been announced. And when you ask yourself practically how is all this going to work . . . they say "we don't know." . . . You ask yourself what is decentralization going to do in an empire of different nationalities that has never had decentralization, whose national identity was always bound up with a strong center? You can see major problems ahead.

The Council trip did not alter the course of U.S. relations with the Soviet Union. It did, nonetheless, affirm that Gorbachev was serious and trustworthy and that a major transformation was on the way, at a time when many Americans had not yet made up their minds about his sincerity. Even Kirkpatrick softened her hard-line views about Gorbachev. The visit conveyed to Council members, who taught hundreds of students, ran major businesses looking for investment and trade opportunities abroad, and worked in government to formulate policies in regions that the Soviet Union touched, that Gorbachev's reforms—though they could have an uncertain path—would create unprecedented potential for cooperation.

A NEW WORLD ORDER,
A FAMILIAR COUNCIL

By the close of the decade, the twenty-four-hour cable news cycle was bringing images of constant, global upheaval into American homes. In three short years, from 1989 to 1991, Americans from all walks of life watched the Berlin Wall come down, the Soviet Union dissolve, China violently suppress protesters in Tiananmen Square, Iraq invade Kuwait, and Yugoslavia break apart, ushering in a four-year civil war in Bosnia.

The disappearance of the Soviet Union unleashed an existential crisis at the Council, as it did at many other organizations and institutes, from the State Department to the Brookings Institution and Columbia University's Harriman Institute for Soviet Studies: Who or what will we study now? Is this the end of history or the beginning of a unipolar era dominated by the United States? Is Japan going to be the next rival? How can civil wars end? How do we prevent state collapse? How do we keep Soviet nuclear facilities safe? How do we redefine international organizations?

The Gulf War in 1991 intensified the sense of upheaval, as broadcasts of American forces pushing Iraqi troops out of Kuwait and bombing Baghdad captured the attention of the American public. Yet foreign policy organizations, including the Council, were not positioned to seize the moment and help the public make sense of the turmoil. Nor was the Council able to foster sustained debates on how to shape what George H.W. Bush called a "new world order."

Much of the work seemed reactive, with Council meetings playing back recent international events or offering high-altitude thoughts on global politics: "The Crisis in the Gulf," "What Now for the World Trading System?," "Europe and America: Cooperation or Competition," "The Changing World Order: Rhetoric or Reality?" But such

People sitting on the Berlin Wall as it begins to be dismantled, 1989

events were not much different from what was offered at other foreign policy think tanks, and the Council struggled to devise programs on both short-term management of international crises and long-range changes that could affect American foreign policy.

The Council tried to react as best it could, but it had invested a large part of its work into understanding a world organized around two superpowers and, for the better part of two decades, coasted on its historic reputation. This would not be enough in answering critical questions about foreign policy: What is to be the role of the United States in a post–Cold War world? If the U.S.-USSR rivalry is at an end, how should the United States conduct itself? Should U.S. forces be stationed overseas in Europe and Korea now that the Cold War is over? How best can the United States create and support alliances with the nations of Europe and the Pacific Rim while entering a period of intense cooperation and competition?

In his remaining time as Council president, Tarnoff created a Task Force on Minority Members to bring a diversity of people and views to the Council, added a science and technology fellowship, and

98

published a survey, *Sea-Changes: American Foreign Policy in a World Transformed*, in which seventeen experts showed how global relations were "on the brink of fundamental transformation." But the changes were not systemic or substantive enough to capture the attention of policymakers, particularly in an ecosystem that was populated with more think tanks. Some, such as Brookings and the Hoover Institution, had old roots similar to the Council, while others, such as the Atlantic Council, the Center for Strategic and International Studies, the Wilson Center, and the Peterson Institute for International Economics, had been formed during the Cold War. As the number of think tanks grew, policymakers and the foreign policy–minded public had the luxury of choosing from a menu of products and events across different venues. And with more think tanks doing work in foreign policy, competition over funding intensified.

Compounding the problem, the Council's finances were in bad shape. Subscriptions to the Corporate Program were lagging, and member contributions to the annual fund were lackluster. Even Board members were tough to rally, with fewer than half donating.

Facing page top: President George H.W. Bush addressing Congress

Facing page bottom: CFR President Peter Tarnoff (right) with Cyrus Vance and Henry Kissinger

PART THREE

A NEW COUNCIL
EMERGES

1993–2021

OCTOBER 23, 1995

n a city of thousands of restaurants, Fidel Castro could not get a reservation. "He was a terribly unpopular guy," Leslie H. Gelb recalled. "He had no invitations to speak. Even restaurants wouldn't accept him as a diner, because they were afraid to be picketed." Gelb, who succeeded Tarnoff as the Council's president in 1993, invited Castro to speak at a breakfast meeting and a dinner event hosted by David Rockefeller. It happened to be on the same day that many world leaders were in New York and passing through the Council, including the Palestinian leader Yasir Arafat and Uzbekistan's President Islam Karimov.

The roster of leaders visiting the Council revealed how much the world had changed. Fifteen new republics had replaced the Soviet Union. Karimov was at the helm of a country fewer than five years old and getting a fair amount of attention from American energy companies and corporations eager to learn about investment opportunities. Arafat had revamped his image, having stood on the White House lawn in 1993 next to Israeli Prime Minister Yitzhak Rabin and U.S. President Bill Clinton for the signing of the Oslo Peace Accords. Castro was in crisis mode, presiding over a growing economic collapse after the country had lost huge subsidies and aid from Moscow.

Castro, grateful that the organization received him at a time when no other venue would, invited Gelb to visit Cuba later that year.

After landing at Havana's airport, Gelb was whisked away to a lake house encircled by a large fence. As soon as Gelb entered the house, he turned to the first wall and said, "I hope when Castro has us to dinner in a couple nights, his gift for me is a box of Cohiba Lanceros." Gelb was a cigar aficionado in those days, and over the course of his stay he repeated his wish in front of every wall in the house. Cuba being an authoritarian country, he figured, someone would be listening.

At the dinner with Castro, the discussion gave way to a fierce debate when the Cuban leader claimed America was not a democracy.

"Why aren't we a democracy?" Gelb asked.

"Because there's no majority rule in your country," Castro said. "A majority of the people want to have relations with Cuba, and your government keeps blocking it."

"You know, you're right," Gelb replied. "Our democracy is minorities rule. Our minorities rule—on Social Security the elderly, or on guns the gun lobby, or on Israel or Middle East issues the Jewish lobby, and Greece the Greek lobby, and on Cuba the Cuba lobby. That's how we work."

"Aha!" Castro said. "You see? I said you're a dictatorship and not a democracy."

Gelb said, "No, no, you're the dictatorship. We're the democracy, because we can actually change our minorities that rule. The Cuban people can't do that."

The conversation continued to other subjects, and Gelb started fidgeting from nicotine withdrawal. Castro stopped speaking and looked at Gelb. "Don't worry. You'll get your Cohibas." An assistant brought a box of cigars, and Castro scribbled something on a card and slipped it inside.

Back in his room, Gelb opened the box and read the message: "Good luck getting this through U.S. Customs."

A FRESH START

Gelb was an unusual choice for a Council president. On the one hand, he was a familiar face, having worked on various Council studies since the 1970s and published in *Foreign Affairs* on Vietnam, and he had served in the Department of Defense under McNamara and as Carter's assistant secretary of state. On the other hand, his more recent background as a hard-hitting national security correspondent for the *New York Times* made him a potential liability, and he had written articles that did little to ingratiate him with people in power. The titles screamed trouble: "Right-Wing Myths," "Mr. Bush's Fateful Blunder," "Where's Mr. Bush?," and "Why the Democrats Don't Look Ready for the White House." He had even gone after fellow writers, calling them "journalistic cannibals." When asked why the Council would choose him as its president given how many people he had lambasted, Gelb laughed and said, "Yes, it puzzled me too."

But in 1993, Gelb was keen on the opportunity. America was at an unusual moment in its history. It needed to redefine foreign policy at a time when the Cold War centerpiece on which it was based had disappeared. Foreign policy was still operating on principles of containment, but, with the Soviet Union gone, it had lost its purpose. As Gelb saw it, many liberals thought that an era of peace was at hand while many conservatives had not gotten their bearings yet. "They hadn't found a new enemy, and it was one of those real periods of germination, intellectual challenge, and I thought it would be an enormous opportunity to try to get hold of an institution like this and go through that process in a very serious way," he said.

Facing page: CFR President Leslie H. Gelb

He spent weeks preparing for his twelve-minute presentation to the search committee. On the day of the interview, he told the committee that he intended the job to be the capstone of his career. He would hold it long enough to transform the place.

> I knew that everybody on that search committee, every serious person connected with the Council, wanted this place transformed, because it had become sleepy, and some even thought it was dead. . . . The Council, like every other foreign policy organization, had lost its way without the Cold War. There wasn't much interest in foreign affairs. It wasn't even clear what international relations was all about anymore.

Jeane Kirkpatrick, vice chair, was keen on Gelb to lead the Council. She vouched for his seriousness and nonpartisanship immediately after his presentation. But a small core of members was firmly opposed, in part because they liked the Council's programs, the profile of its members, and its culture as it was, even if they admitted that the Council needed to change somehow. As head of the search committee, Peter G. Peterson moved quickly to solidify support among directors who liked Gelb's vision, and he neutralized the opposition by assuring worried Board members that the Council would be better for all the changes.

Gelb got the job and laid out his plan in a strategy paper. He did not wish to restructure radically, but significant adjustments had to be made to restore the Council. He outlined several goals: put the Council on the cutting edge of foreign policy thinking, expand national outreach, and nurture the next generation of foreign policy leaders. Gelb explained why this was necessary by referring to the foreign policy context.

Much of the new policy context was old—regional rivalries, nationalism, and such—but some new subjects required serious attention, including the spread of democracy, the broader role of the United Nations, the shifting of global economic power toward Asia, the rise of terrorism, outbreaks of civil and ethnic conflict, and new global norms on human rights. To meaningfully cover these areas, he would have to broaden membership because, as he wrote in the strategy paper, "younger fellows may be better equipped than the Cold War generation to see the emerging outlines of world politics." Gelb promised that these and other changes would reestablish one of the

Council's most important functions: "to help officials think privately about policy options."

Some Board members tried to hit the brakes, including Paul Volcker, former chair of the Federal Reserve and member of CFR's Finance and Budget Committee. Volcker told Gelb the strategy would wreck the organization; Volcker enjoyed the clubby atmosphere of the past and was known for pulling out a cigar at Council events. He was a fan of the old Council and its atmosphere, and, at six foot seven, his gruff exterior could easily intimidate. Gelb did not waver.

Neither did his allies, particularly Peterson, who was determined to work closely with Gelb to change the Council to make it younger, more dynamic, and more impactful to policymakers and the public. Peterson remembered attending one meeting with Gelb in those first weeks:

> The average age had to be in the seventies, with half of those seemingly asleep. I remember walking out, and the two of us saying, "We have to do something about this." And Les, who has a great sense of humor, said that this is the only organization he knew that when you died you didn't have to pay dues, but you could continue to attend meetings.

Over the years, Gelb worked closely with Peterson and his enthusiasts on the Board to push ahead with his vision. Among them was Maurice R. Greenberg, who joined the Board after Jeane Kirkpatrick stepped down in 1994. Greenberg also became chair of the Finance Committee. Gelb, Peterson, and Greenberg made for an intimate troika, pushing through many changes, some transformative, some painful. It was a different way to run the Council, one that empowered core Board members and gave Gelb tremendous authority to implement his vision. Greenberg admitted, "If we'd met and had a talk about an issue—and we met frequently—Peterson, myself, and Les, we came to conclusions very, very quickly. You didn't have to sit and debate and ruminate and hypothecate and delay, and that fit my personality just perfectly."

Gelb pushed through many changes in his first years. He revitalized the Term Member Program in 1994, bringing in one hundred

Joan Spero (right) with John G. Heimann, 1993

new, younger members in the first couple years, and he created a Task Force that would search for ways to make the Council more diverse. He recruited more women to the Board, including Joan Spero, a former international affairs fellow who had done a pioneering study of the finance industry at the New York Federal Reserve Bank under Volcker. Gelb called Spero one day to ask her to run for the Board. "Do you think I have a chance of winning?" she asked. "Probably not," he replied, "but I think you'd be great, so I want you to run." Spero lost the first election but managed to win enough votes for a seat on the Board a couple years later.

Spero laughed about Gelb being "warm and cuddly," and some younger staff found him to be a wonderful mentor. But he could also be mercurial and blunt. He was irritated with staff who treated Fridays as optional work days. "There was nobody here after noon on Fridays any given day. The place was deserted," he said. "So I used to go around most of the Fridays and just leave notes on everybody's desk who wasn't there."

His hand was particularly heavy with the directors of Studies. During his ten years at the Council, Gelb went through seven directors, the same number that the Council had had in its entire history before him. Even senior fellows felt pressured, as Gelb admitted to telling some, "If what you're saying in these books is so new, important, and different, how come it hasn't already been done?" Gelb wanted the Council to have a successful Studies Program and a line of influ-ential books, but he equally wanted to be his own director of Studies. One staff member who worked in Studies at the time remarked with a laugh that the only way to survive this period was to work on a project that Gelb did not care about.

Some changes caused uproars that even Peterson and Greenberg could not contain. Gelb decided to end the Council's relationship with the Committees on Foreign Relations that had proliferated across the country. In his view, the committees were loosely organized and incohesive and did not serve a clear benefit to the Council. Some staff members disagreed. They saw the committees as a good way for the Council to better understand how different parts of the United States saw foreign policy. But Gelb had made up his mind, and he preferred to devote the Council's energies to expanding its own national mem-bership. He dispatched Alton Frye to deliver the bad news. The com-mittees were stunned, and there was a lot of anger among their ranks at the way it was done. Council staff who had spent years working with the committees were similarly upset.

Another change Gelb sought with Peterson's blessing was to expand the range of voices at the Council by bringing in non-Americans as associate members. This idea would have been a major departure from the founding principles of the Council. The world had changed seventy years later, however, becoming deeply interconnected. Gelb and Peter-son drafted a letter explaining their intention after conferring with the Membership Committee.

A large contingent of members balked. "They thought that this was bringing in the aliens, who were going to destroy planet earth," Gelb said. Letters of strong support came from members such as Reagan's Secretary of Defense Caspar W. Weinberger and Paul Nitze, who had worked in several administrations during the Cold War shaping defense strategy; they thought a foreign perspective would enrich policy discussions. However, major opposition came from members who thought that the initiative would undermine the Council's focus on American foreign policy or make American policymakers reluc-tant to speak openly at Council meetings. And a core of the Council's Black members wanted Gelb to first increase the number of members from minority groups in America before looking outside the coun-try to expand membership. Gelb's proposal failed. In lieu of having non-American members, the Council would assemble an Interna-tional Advisory Board of prominent non-Americans who would occa-sionally advise the Council on its programs.

Despite occasional setbacks, Gelb continued to work closely with Peterson and Greenberg to expand the Council's work. The Center for Preventive Action was established in 1994 to better understand how to mitigate conflicts and crises, such as ethnic cleansing, civil war, and state failure, that were proliferating. In 1995, the same year as the Castro visit, an Independent Task Force series was launched to examine pressing policy issues and present bipartisan policy recommendations.

The Task Forces were particularly important in correcting what Gelb saw as past missteps. Gelb believed that Vietnam had split the foreign policy community, ideologically and politically:

> Not that there weren't differences before—there obviously were. People had very strong arguments about the best way of containing the Soviet Union, the Acheson-Kennan debates. They were fierce, but they were substantive, very good. . . . Things got more and more political, more and more personal, and we went from a world where there were a handful of foreign policy think tanks to dozens of them, each representing a different point along the political-ideological spectrum. Foreign policy experts became warriors, essentially, and there was very little give and take . . . and you see that in the larger political arena, where almost nobody will support the policy of anybody else, let alone the policy of the other part. It's not that there weren't people who were always partisan—there were. But there were also a lot of people who would move from one side to the other depending upon how they saw the national interest. The foreign policy community just became too split to do that on many occasions. I had hoped that the Task Forces would help to overcome that problem.

The first Task Forces tackled the hot-button subjects of nuclear proliferation, NATO expansion, and the U.S.-North Korean nuclear accord. Task Force members were selected to include subject experts and people affiliated with both Republican and Democratic administrations. As of 2020, the Council has sponsored seventy-eight Task Forces and counting, and their reports represent an important expansion of the Council's work in presenting nonpartisan policy options.

One of the best examples of this work was on an issue that typically attracted the most partisan and acrimonious debates. The

Refugees fleeing from the former Yugoslavia

report of a 2001 Independent Task Force, *U.S.-Cuban Relations in the 21st Century*, codirected by Julia E. Sweig and Walter Russell Mead, recommended that the United States prepare for the next stage in U.S.-Cuban relations by taking cautious steps, such as permitting the sale of agricultural and medical products and allowing all Americans to travel to Cuba. "The point of the Task Force's work was never for Havana to like it," explained Peterson. "The objective was to prompt new thinking, in Washington, in Miami, and on the island itself. The Task Force did just that."

Shortly after, a Council delegation that included Peterson, Sweig, Rockefeller, and Board member Carla A. Hills visited Havana. The delegation had many memorable and tough conversations with Cuban officials, according to Peterson:

> Virtually every member of our delegation and every senior Cuban official we met cited proposals in the two reports of the Council-sponsored Independent Task Force on Cuba. Not that the Cubans were positive: Just before

NATO ENLARGEMENT

STABILITY AND SECURITY IN THE 21st CENTURY

our visit, state television devoted much of its prime-time schedule on three consecutive nights to criticism of the Task Force's work. And in our meetings, President Fidel Castro and other top Cuban officials pulled no punches in confronting our group with their objections to many of the Task Force's recommendations.

In Havana, Hills was stunned to learn that the man who helped her with her luggage was a full-time doctor moonlighting to make extra money. It was an ugly contrast with the lavish dinner Castro had hosted—Dom Pérignon bottles on the table. The trip also reinforced her beliefs that universal sanctions do not work. Hills said, "A fifty-year universal sanction is fifty years of never, never, ever working," and it was time to find a new way ahead. Reflecting on the importance of the Task Force and the Council's work, Gelb explained, "We were dealing with adversaries we considered far more threatening to American security than Fidel Castro, and the only reason we weren't dealing with him was the result of American domestic politics."

Facing page top: *President Bill Clinton signs a document notifying NATO of U.S. approval of its expansion.*

Facing page bottom: *Robert Wilmers and Peter G. Peterson meet Fidel Castro in Havana.*

RENOVATING THE MAGAZINE

Huge changes had been taking place at *Foreign Affairs*. During the early years of the Cold War, the magazine had been the sole place to publish policy-driven pieces on international affairs. When someone like Zbigniew Brzezinski wanted to do a policy-relevant piece on U.S.-Soviet relations, CFR member and Soviet expert Robert Legvold explained, "*Foreign Affairs* was it. Nowhere else. There was no *Washington Quarterly*. There was no *Foreign Policy* magazine. There was no *Orbis*. There were none of these other lesser lights, and, even if they had existed, they would have still chosen *Foreign Affairs* because by now it had clout and cachet." No longer the only game in town, the magazine had been facing huge competition for readers and contributors and was overdue for a makeover.

In 1992, William G. Hyland retired, and Peter Grose stepped down as managing editor. Hyland went on to write a biography of George Gershwin and the Jazz Age, while Grose wrote a biography of Allen Dulles. In Hyland's place, the Council hired James F. Hoge Jr. Hoge had distinguished himself as a journalist and editor in chief at the *Chicago Sun-Times* and later president and publisher of the *New York Daily News*. But he needed a managing editor with a solid command of international affairs. Walter Isaacson, an accomplished biographer and editor at *Time* magazine, would help him find one.

Isaacson met a twenty-eight-year-old Harvard graduate student over lunch and suggested that he apply for the position at *Foreign Affairs*. Isaacson knew Hoge and thought the student, Fareed Zakaria, would complement Hoge's skills well. Zakaria said, "It is very nice of you to think of me, but I have no interest in it. I think I am going to end up getting a job at Harvard, and I do not want to go off and be an editor at *Foreign Affairs* if I can be a professor at Harvard." That evening, Zakaria thought to himself, "Gosh, why did I say that?" He called Isaacson to say that he had changed his mind.

At the interview, Zakaria laid out his ideas for the magazine. His predecessor, Grose, had far more experience and had been one of the chief diplomatic correspondents of the *New York Times*. According to Zakaria, Hoge was "a little unnerved about the prospect of this twenty-eight-year-old glorified graduate student who was urging a revolution." Zakaria suggested Hoge give him a chance to redo the current issue of the magazine as a demonstration. He recounted,

> So I took that quarter's issue of *Foreign Affairs*, and I killed, I think, four of the articles out of ten, and I drastically reedited three or four of them. . . . Most were seven thousand words or more. I cut them back to four thousand words . . . drastically changed them, reordered them, in some cases actually rewrote whole pages, and said, "This is, I think, what the author is trying to say, and if we can get him to say this, it would make for a better piece."

Hoge offered Zakaria the job.

Hoge and Zakaria were a good tandem as publisher and academic, and they instituted major changes that revived the magazine: they added article summaries to help busy readers choose which articles to read, added a comments section and expanded the reviews, and ruthlessly cut the word limit for essays from eight-to-twelve thousand to four-to-five thousand words. Some writers were outraged that their articles were being radically shortened, but "readers, by and large, were happy," Zakaria said. The greatest changes Hoge and Zakaria instituted were in the content, and the first redesigned issue in 1993 created a major, global splash.

In the spring of 1993, Zakaria approached his advisor at Harvard, Samuel Huntington, to publish one of his draft articles in *Foreign Affairs*. The odds were not in Zakaria's favor both because Huntington was disappointed that Zakaria had left academia and because he had promised his article to the *National Interest*. Zakaria persisted, and Huntington agreed.

"The Clash of Civilizations?" ended up being the most cited, reprinted, and translated piece in *Foreign Affairs* history. It argued that the main causes of conflict in the future would revolve around civilizational identity, and Huntington singled out Islam as the civilization

Madeleine K. Albright with editors of Foreign Affairs: *(left to right) James F. Hoge Jr., William Bundy, and William G. Hyland*

most likely to see conflict at its borders with the West and internally between Sunnis and Shias. Readers loved it or hated it, but few found themselves unaffected by Huntington's argument. The article jolted policymakers in the United States and abroad. "After we printed that piece," Hoge said, "the American ambassador in Indonesia—the largest Muslim country in the world—sent a flash telegram to the State Department saying, 'Please send somebody out here to counteract this argument. The place is aflame.'"

Then onward, many *Foreign Affairs* articles were written to provoke—not for the sake of controversy but to trigger healthy debates. In the same issue as the "The Clash of Civilizations?," John Mearsheimer, a professor at the University of Chicago and a leading realist voice, wrote a piece urging Ukraine to keep its nuclear weapons rather than transfer them to Russia. The article alarmed advocates of disarmament and many other foreign policy experts, yet Russia's absorption of Crimea and intervention in eastern Ukraine decades later indicates the piece perhaps deserved more consideration than the critics gave it.

During the 1990s, most policymakers found it difficult to ignore the magazine, and subscriptions consistently stayed above one hundred thousand. After the magazine had run several pieces on the dual containment program—designed to constrain Iran and Iraq—Hoge got a call from Madeleine K. Albright, secretary of state in the second Clinton administration. "Jim, we got the message," Albright said. "You don't need to do another piece. We got the message. We're not changing our policy." Albright may have been irked by the article, but she also understood that this was the nature of the mission of *Foreign Affairs* and the Council—to deliver nonpartisan analysis of foreign policy on its own terms. She would go on to author articles in *Foreign Affairs*, participate in Council meetings and Task Forces, and serve on the Board of Directors.

CFR AT Y2K

I n 1997, the Council had moved into a larger space in Washington, DC. The centerpiece of the work in Washington was a project that Alton Frye led: the Congress and U.S. Foreign Policy program. The timing was right, as the Clinton administration was at loggerheads with Republicans in Congress and few constructive conversations were taking place across party lines. This dynamic struck Gelb and Frye as wrong, and Frye designed a Council series for congressional staff working on challenging foreign policy issues. Following one meeting, a Republican and a Democratic staffer were amiably continuing the topic of conversation in the hallway. Frye remembers a third staffer walking by, stunned to see them talking. "There was a surprise that these political adversaries could have found a place where they could have a civil discourse," he said. This role of the Council as a unique, nonpartisan space on the Hill continues today.

Also in 1997, the Council launched its website, CFR.org, and inaugurated a new International Affairs Fellowship in Japan, sponsored by Hitachi. But other work was unfolding more slowly, presenting the Council with greater challenges, none more than the question of diversity and minority representation. The son of Hungarian Jewish immigrants, Gelb worked his way through school washing dishes and had seen his share of prejudice. He cared deeply about diversity, and bringing underrepresented racial and ethnic groups into the Council was one of the pillars of his vision. George A. Dalley, a Council member and chair of the Task Force on Minorities, was blunt about the Council's need for greater diversity:

> Minority group members of the Council know they are
> not receiving all the benefits of Council membership.

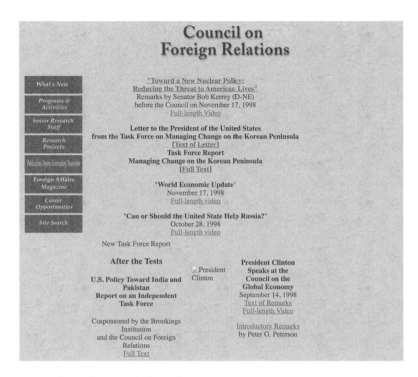

A screenshot of the Council's first website, 1997

They believe the reasons for their lack of greater
engagement in the work of the Council are part of
the lack of effort by the staff of the Council to recognize their expertise, and thus include them in activities such as study groups, and in part their reluctance
to attend Council events at which they are usually the
only minority, and there is no effort made to welcome
or engage in conversation by other Council members
during the social period.

Donald McHenry, Board member and frequent presider at Council meetings, had a somewhat different view of the matter:

The staff of the Council has to be as representative as
we want the membership to be, and to the extent that we
don't do that then we will inevitably fail. The tendency is
for those who set up a study group on whatever the subject is to include . . . the people that they know, and if they

don't know them, they don't get included. So the inclusiveness of the Council comes up short.

Gelb was disappointed that the numbers of racial and ethnic minority members at the Council had plateaued. He wrote to the Board in July 1997 expressing his disappointment and reminded them that at the beginning of his presidency he had promised, "We will bring greater diversity to Council affairs, not for diversity's sake, but for our own sake." But few nonminority members were nominating minorities for membership, and the Council was not making enough progress to incorporate the concerns and interests of Black and Latinx members.

Frustrations with the lack of inclusion and representation would surface periodically, even in areas that Gelb did not initially see as related to diversity and inclusion. For example, Gelb felt great regret that the Council had not done more work on Rwanda when he observed the Clinton administration look the other way as a genocide was taking place. It took him years to get money together to endow a senior fellowship in African affairs despite having ten or eleven other endowed chairs at the Council. Once the money was raised, he convened a meeting in Washington, DC, with fifty people in a room and twenty on the telephone. He proudly announced his idea to name the chair after Nelson Mandela, and immediately people started protesting, "What do you mean, you can't find an African American in America to name it after? You have to name it after an African?"

What had been envisioned as the Nelson Mandela chair in 2003 became the Ralph Bunche chair in Africa policy studies, the first chair of its kind in any foreign policy think tank or school. Bunche was a political scientist and diplomat and had received the 1950 Nobel Peace Prize for his mediation efforts in the Arab-Israeli conflict. Bunche had been one of the Council's first Black members, joining in 1949. He would go on to participate in the civil rights movement, including the 1963 March on Washington with Martin Luther King Jr. and the 1965 marches from Selma to Montgomery.

The Council would make more consequential changes around the millennium. One was to relax the confidentiality requirements for some of its meetings and discussions to make it a more public institution.

With exceptions that were few and far between—Clemenceau's address in 1928 at the Met Opera, Dulles's massive retaliation remarks in 1953, and occasional broadcast initiatives such as the radio show *America and the World* with author and journalist Kati I. Marton—the Council was true to its identity as a private, membership organization.

The magazine, books, and opinion pieces fellows produced were necessarily public and intended to make a mark on policy, but the Council's proceedings, meetings, and discussions were confidential or at least bound by nonattributive rules.

What Council members saw as a matter of privacy some outsiders interpreted as nefarious secrecy. Over the decades, the Council became a favorite target of conspiracy theorists. Some alleged that the Council had a Bolshevik agenda, including a letter writer in the 1950s who simply addressed the envelope in bold red letters to: "C.F.R.— Cowards for Russia, New York." A more popular conspiracy theory in the 1970s accused the Council and the Trilateral Commission of controlling American foreign policy.

Ralph Bunche joined the Council in 1949 and had a chair named in his honor in 2003.

"If only we were so lucky," joked some members. Robert Legvold remembered looking into a particularly colorful theory that linked the Council to an intergalactic conspiracy: Back in 1954, Eisenhower met secretly with aliens in Morocco, and they appointed the first extraterrestrial ambassador to the United States. With the help of the Council, the government was keeping the alien invasion a secret from the American people.

The internet age provided the Council an opportunity to become more public, not as a response to conspiracy theories but to reach broader audiences and become more dynamic. In 1999, the Council took a step in this direction when it inaugurated Peterson Hall, a new room at Pratt House outfitted with the latest videoconferencing and communications technology, thanks to a gift from Peterson. Before long, the Council was hitting new digital milestones: the first study group meeting over videoconference, the first live webcast of a general meeting, and the first videos posted to the new website. Interest in the Council among conspiracy theorists waned for a while.

An LP alleging CFR ties to a shadowy
international group, one of many such
conspiratorial publications targeting CFR
over the years

Peterson explained that he intended his gift to help the Council reach a "truly national, involved membership," and this meant understanding what "people in Texas and California and the Red states think about foreign policy." His sentiment overlapped with Gelb's desire to revive the National Program and bring more voices from around the country into the Council fold. By the new millennium, the Council counted 3,988 members, divided nearly evenly among New York, Washington, DC, and the rest of the country.

The Council started the twenty-first century with a parade of new work: It revamped the Center for Preventive Action with more money and programs. By virtue of a major gift from Greenberg, it created the Center for Geoeconomic Studies to produce smart, economically driven work about foreign policy that was not bogged down with academic jargon and that reflected how globalization had fundamentally changed the world.

It launched the Campaign 2000 website to highlight foreign policy issues in the presidential contest between Al Gore and George W. Bush and has continued to do so for every presidential election since. And in a year in which Bush occasionally stumped in Spanish to court Latinx voters, *Foreign Affairs* published its first edition in Spanish.

The Council and the magazine ramped up coverage of China in this period. Elizabeth C. Economy, a senior fellow, directed a study group on China and the environment, while *Foreign Affairs* published articles on a range of issues such as Beijing's nuclear weapons program, its growing cyber power, trade relations, and tensions in the Taiwan Strait. It was a sign of how fast foreign policy themes can change that fears about Japan outpacing the United States were given over to worries that Japan was not independent enough in its foreign policy and not helpful in countering China.

One of the best examples was political scientist and China expert Andrew J. Nathan's "The Tiananmen Papers" in *Foreign Affairs*. The article infuriated Chinese officials by revealing secret decisions they had made to quash the 1989 demonstrations. Internet firewalls were still remedial in 2001, and China's censors had to play a game of whack-a-mole to suppress the documents. Just when they took down one portal, students would find another to post the article and accompanying documents. To the Council's credit, directors who had major business interests in China never tried to interfere with the magazine's operation, and the magazine continued to foster an honest and open discussion on foreign policy no matter whom it offended. It was a reminder of the long-standing policy at the Council to respect the editorial independence of the magazine.

A Spanish-language edition of Foreign Affairs, *one of several foreign-language versions of the magazine published at various times*

SEPTEMBER 11, 2001

Acrid smoke filled the air of lower Manhattan as the remains of the World Trade Center smoldered. The haze and smell eventually made its way uptown. People at the Council were stunned, confused, frightened, angry, defiant—a mix of emotions that most Americans felt on that day and in the months that followed.

Gelb rallied the staff and directors to confront the new reality. "America's response to terrorism—be prepared, not scared" became the thread across Council programming, and several Task Forces were put together. The following year, the Council launched a Terrorism Q and A website and an Outreach program to better inform people, who now saw that foreign policy mattered in their daily lives in ways they might not have imagined before the attacks. Initial work debated how to rout al-Qaeda and the Taliban in Afghanistan, how best to protect America, and how the country could build enduring alliances in the war on terror.

Before long, it became clear that the Bush administration was intent on taking the war to Iraq, a decision that Richard Haass would characterize as an ill-advised war of choice.

During a jam-packed Council meeting on January 23, 2003, Deputy Secretary of Defense Paul Wolfowitz felt the heat when one member criticized the administration's march to war: "You are not presenting us with any credible evidence, and we think there are a lot of Americans who will approach this subject in the same way." Peterson remembered Wolfowitz appearing chastened. Few institutions would challenge him so directly, and he had already been infuriated by *Foreign Affairs* articles such as "The Rollback Fantasy" and "The Exit Strategy Delusion," which challenged his worldview.

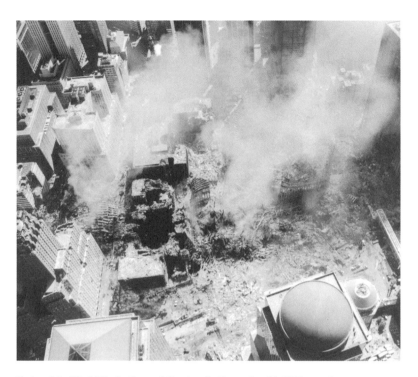

Ruins of the World Trade Center following the September 11, 2001, attacks

Yet, Gelb was a cheerleader for the Iraq War. He supported the invasion so long as the United States was prepared to stay the course and have a clear plan for the task of postconflict transition and reconstruction. As he saw it, if the U.S. government was determined to pursue war, the Council could be of use in planning for the day after. "Before the war started, I called Condi Rice and Steve Hadley [Bush's national security advisor and CFR member]," Gelb said, "and suggested . . . that we would pull together a Task Force with two other foreign policy think tanks on postwar planning for Iraq." At a meeting in Condoleezza Rice's office, Christopher DeMuth from the American Enterprise Institute asked if the president, Deputy Chief of Staff Karl Rove, and Defense Secretary Donald Rumsfeld were aware of the idea. Gelb remembered DeMuth saying, "This sounds like a nation-building exercise, and we're against nation-building in this administration. All of you gave speeches that we can't do nation-building. It was one of the big mistakes of the Clinton administration."

U.S. troops in Tikrit, Iraq, 2003

Rice tried to defend the proposal as an information exercise and made the case that the Council, together with other institutions, could bring in far more expertise than the government. It was not meant to be. "Two weeks later, Steve Hadley called me up and said the idea was junked," Gelb said. "But that would have been the Council at its very best. The need was very clear." Instead, the Council would issue reports such as *Iraq: The Day After* and cosponsor a study, "Guiding Principles for U.S. Post-Conflict Policy in Iraq," with the James A. Baker III Institute for Public Policy. Although the reports were thorough and warned of the troubles that would follow in Iraq if the United States did not prepare for the task of reconstruction and state-building, they did not have the participation or buy-in with Bush administration officials Gelb had hoped for, and this limited their impact.

Gelb was disappointed, and leading the Council for a decade had been exacting. During his tenure, he also refrained from writing. In the 1990s, soon after joining the Council, Gelb wrote a piece in the *Washington Post* criticizing the Clinton administration for masquerading its domestic policy as foreign policy. "I got somewhere between two hundred and three hundred letters of protest about the thing," Gelb said. He had been proud of the argument, but the reaction worried him—would policymakers and the public mistake his writing for a Council position? He waited nearly a decade before publishing another controversial piece, after stepping down as Council president. In "The Three-State Solution," Gelb called for a partition of Iraq. The idea became the basis for then Senator Joe Biden's Iraq plan after Gelb engrossed him in a three-hour conversation when their flight to Washington, DC, was delayed on the tarmac at LaGuardia Airport.

Gelb had transformed the Council. A $750,000 deficit turned into a $2 million surplus, membership increased 50 percent and became younger on average, meetings became far livelier, and Harold Pratt Associates, the Council's group of major donors, quadrupled. Greenberg summed up the Gelb years, "I think you have to look at what was achieved and where we came from, in order to put it in perspective. . . . The Council was kind of dreary for a long time, and Gelb did liven it up, and as a manager he did reach out and bring fresh blood in, and he did raise more money than was done previously. . . . [He was] a catalyst for change, and he did very well."

At the same time, waking up the Council came at a cost. Gelb combined power and supreme confidence. He scorned conventional wisdom and had strong opinions about many areas of foreign policy. When he did not like the results of a study group on the Persian Gulf, he did another one.

Gelb overhauled the Studies Program, the intellectual heart of the Council. When he arrived in the early 1990s, the Council had twenty fellows and two endowed chairs. When he stepped down, there were seventy fellows and twelve endowed chairs. Yet, relative to the huge amounts of money that Board members were pouring into the Council, Gelb missed an opportunity to greatly improve the substance and influence of the Studies Program, which now had more peers and competitors across the think-tank landscape.

In part because of the high turnover in directors, fellows were spending too much time convening roundtables and study groups for members, and too few books were coming out of Studies, notwithstanding the quality of volumes such as Jagdish Bhagwati's *In Defense of Globalization*—which won *BusinessWeek*'s Best Book of the Year award—Yoichi Funabashi's first-class diplomatic history *Alliance Adrift*, or Richard Haass's *The Reluctant Sheriff: The United States After the Cold War*. And the program was doing too little to disseminate the books to audiences who most needed to read them and thereby missing the opportunity to shape foreign policy debates.

Overall, Gelb and a core of Board members determined much of what the Council did or did not do. This could feel deflating to senior staff who were experts in foreign policy and had their own ideas about initiatives the Council could take on. Though Gelb had restored the Council and expanded its work, the Council was also ready for new leadership and a new vision.

REBOOTING THE COUNCIL

February 23, 2019—"Foreign policy is too important to be left to the diplomats." It was a surprising statement from an accomplished ambassador and former head of policy planning at the State Department. But Richard Haass, president of the Council on Foreign Relations since 2003, wanted to get his point across to the twenty-nine governors assembled at the National Governors Association meeting.

The theme of the meeting was the future of work, and Haass was speaking on the opening panel alongside Penny Pritzker, who had been the secretary of commerce in the Obama administration. A CFR Independent Task Force report issued months earlier, *The Work Ahead: Machines, Skills, and U.S. Leadership in the Twenty-First Century,* had warned that as many as one-third of American workers could need to change occupations and acquire new skills by 2030 if the automation of work continued to rise. Black Americans were particularly susceptible to losing jobs because of their concentration in occupations affected by automation. These worrying trends were just one indication that the U.S. economy was losing its global edge and historic resilience that made the American model so appealing around the world. As the report pointed out, in 1970 more than 90 percent of thirty-year-olds earned more than their parents had at the same age; by 2019, that number was down to nearly 50 percent.

Steve Bullock, the Democratic governor of Montana and panel chair, asked, "How do we make sure Americans aren't left behind in a changing world?"

"It's the right question; it's the right issue," Haass answered. "It's the reason why we had this Task Force. The stakes here are enormous. . . . You ain't seen nothing yet. The amount of jobs that will be displaced

*Governor Steve Bullock of Montana with Penny Pritzker and Richard N. Haass at the
National Governors Association meeting, 2019*

by the new technologies will be great. While the new tech will create a
lot of new jobs, the mismatch between the skill levels the jobs require
and existing skills of the existing workforce is large. Unless we close that
gap, we are going to have massive social problems. We aren't going to
have the bandwidth we need to deal with foreign policy issues that we
need to deal with. What is going to make this really bad is that this is
going to hit us gradually."

The panelists' assessments were grim. "If we don't have economic
prosperity, we can't have economic competitiveness, and our national
security is at stake," Pritzker told the assembled officials.

Haass later added that chronic and prolonged unemployment of
a displaced workforce would deepen social polarization, decimate
the tax basis that funds infrastructure and the social safety net, and
dramatically affect the ability of the American people to cope with
the changing nature of globalization. He concluded, "We will end up
being much more isolationist if we don't get this right."

But the panel made it clear that the problem could be fixed as long
as state and local officials did not wait for the federal government
to fix it for them. "Do not underestimate the power of your voice on
this issue," Haass told the governors, and he suggested a number of

policy options—relaxing licensing restrictions that prevent people from moving their jobs from one state to another and redirecting budgets to provide more educational opportunities for workers later in life, when they need to learn new skills or change careers because of displacement.

The governors in attendance —some taking notes studiously, others asking questions— seemed to acknowledge that in the twenty-first century, if they wished to ensure their states' future prosperity, diplomacy was their purview as well.

The event was another sign that a decade and a half of investments in a new Outreach strategy had matured. The Council was reaching a much larger number

The Work Ahead, *a 2018 Task Force report that focused on how to rebuild the links among work, opportunity, and economic security in the face of accelerating change*

of Americans beyond the typical foreign policy circles. In doing so, the Council had reinvented itself without sacrificing its classic work.

• • •

With the United States at war with Iraq in 2003, Haass's enthusiasm for the George W. Bush administration was dwindling. He had served as head of the policy planning staff at the State Department, roving ambassador for the administration, U.S. envoy to the peace process in Northern Ireland, and coordinator for the future of Afghanistan after 9/11, but he disagreed profoundly with the decision to go to war in Iraq that March. So when Gelb called and asked if he would be interested in putting his name forward for the job of Council president, Haass agreed.

Haass was a scholar-practitioner with decades of experience working in Congress, the Defense and State Departments, and the White House. He had written extensively on and taught international relations at a number of universities. He ran the foreign policy division

at the Brookings Institution during the Clinton years and, for a short spell, was a senior fellow at the Council's Washington office. He fit the mold of what the Council was looking for in a leader. And his references, Brent Scowcroft and Secretary of State Colin Powell, whom Haass worked for during the two Bush presidencies, impressed the search committee.

Haass made one point unequivocally to the Council's search committee. He wanted to be part of the public debate on foreign policy and was not going to be an invisible administrator. He intended to write and speak about issues close to his heart, and he told the Board, "I will only take this job if you understand that I want to be a full participant in that debate."

Haass made good on his promise. In July 2003, shortly after becoming president of the Council, he wrote an article critical of the Bush administration. Joan Spero recalled that "Pete [Peterson] was very upset. . . . I think it was rash of Richard to do that so quickly, and I think Pete overreacted." Other Board members had a more sympathetic take. Former Treasury Secretary and 2007–17 CFR Board Chair Robert E. Rubin thought that the head of the Council should be "a major figure in the national dialogue, because, first place, you've got this tremendous institution that's informing you . . . and secondly, it projects the institution itself, the Council, into the world more effectively." It was an adjustment for members of the Board, and it took some time for them to get used to Haass's public voice.

There were frictions as well over Haass's plan for the Council, and Haass noted that some people on the Board "remembered the past more fondly than they observed the present." Fouad Ajami was one of the leaders of the opposition on the Board, and he tried to prevent Haass from making too many changes, despite assurances Haass had been given when he took the job. Still, having a gadfly like Ajami on the Board had value in that Haass had to carefully explain why the Council needed reform and win over enough Board members to pursue it.

"For all of Les's personality, it was still a pretty staid organization," Haass explained. "It was an institution that was neither in ideal shape nor in crisis. It was a typical tweener, but that perception was not necessarily universally shared." The Council was doing good work, but it was too limited in its approach and speaking to the same people that

---

Facing page: CFR President Richard N. Haass at the 2005 Corporate Conference

Richard N. Haass and former President of South Africa Nelson Mandela in New York, 2005

made up the foreign policy establishment. Gelb had courted a select group of exceedingly generous donors, but the $30 million budget was limiting, and the Studies Program had suffered whiplash from the many changes in directors. The National and Term Member Programs had grown, but the Council was not fully representative of America's racial, ethnic, and geographic diversity.

Still, new projects immediately got underway. Council Special Reports tackled issues that needed serious, timely treatment in the form of punchy policy briefs. Initial titles included Princeton N. Lyman's *Addressing the HIV/AIDS Pandemic*, Charles D. Ferguson's *Preventing Catastrophic Nuclear Terrorism*, and Steven A. Cook and Elizabeth Sherwood-Randall's *Generating Momentum for a New Era in U.S.-Turkey Relations*. Studies was initially reoriented around three issues: America's grand strategy, global governance, and reform in the Arab and Islamic world. The Council also established the HBO History Makers series to understand the contributions prominent individuals made at critical foreign policy junctures. Those profiled included Madeleine Albright, the first female secretary of state; James

Wolfensohn, former president of the World Bank Group; and General Stanley A. McChrystal, former commander of the Joint Special Operations Command. Similar programming followed in the years to come, including the Lessons From History series, which was endowed by David M. Rubenstein, who became chair of the Council's Board in 2017. The series featured practitioners who played pivotal roles in important foreign policy issues and international events. Episodes included lessons from the Iran revolution, the end of apartheid in South Africa, and the state of intelligence after 9/11.

Haass was a firm believer in the wisdom of applied history and sang the virtues of *Thinking in Time: The Uses of History for Decision Makers*, a book by Harvard University's Richard E. Neustadt and Ernest R. May. Haass encouraged Council fellows to channel the lessons of history in their writing, as he often relied on the wisdom of the past during his time in government. He explained, "I used to bring in outsiders often to meet with the secretary of state or meet with the president just to get an outsider's view. Particularly historians. I would find historians more valuable than experts because government has expertise but rarely has historical perspective in the larger sense of the word."

UPDATING THE CLASSICS

O n February 8, 2005, Haass went before the Board to present his strategy for the Council. He had led through learning and listening for a year and a half before drafting his vision for the Council's next stage.

Here, the foreign policy context was critical. He noted that it had been almost a generation since the end of the Cold War, more than fifteen years since the Berlin Wall was pulled down, over three years since the 9/11 attacks, and two years since the beginning of U.S. military operations in Iraq and the rebuilding effort there. President Bush, stressing the promotion of freedom and democracy abroad and elevating the question of how American power and primacy should be directed, had been elected to a second term. Yet, this question had no clear answers, and the country was mired in a difficult and polarized debate on what direction U.S. foreign policy should take.

Haass made the case before the Board that the Council faced its own urgencies and called for change. The need was reflected in surveys that McKinsey & Company and its former Director and CFR Board member Richard N. Foster had conducted with Council members and external audiences. McKinsey interviewed thirty-one leaders from government, media, and industry and reported overwhelmingly positive views of the Council. CFR represented a gold standard, commanded tremendous respect for its nonpartisan mission, and had impressively strong convening power. It was a trusted source for information and analysis, including *Foreign Affairs*, which had been named the most influential media outlet by U.S. opinion leaders the previous year.

But there were challenges ahead. Haass saw the Council's $169 million endowment as insufficient and its $30 million operating budget as limiting the organization's expansion of programs, its ability to attract top talent to run them, and ultimately its impact. Membership dues and the Annual Fund together only covered one-quarter of the budget. There were worries that foundation support would decline, and the Council relied on a few benefactors to sponsor many of its programs.

More worryingly, the Council was not seen as innovative. The McKinsey survey itself had shortcomings, as the people polled were almost exclusively white and male. If those respondents did not see the Council as innovative and far-reaching, how would more diverse audiences see it?

The Council needed to improve and refine its traditional work—the events, meetings, reports, and studies aimed at its members and foreign policy elites. It also needed to reach new audiences, such as religious leaders, state and local officials, nongovernmental organizers, educators, and journalists—constituencies that were not directly involved in the policy process but whose work mattered in the world of diplomacy and in debates on the country's role in the world. Haass was pressing those at the Council to ask two questions: How can we foster a healthy debate on how America could direct its power and primacy? Whom, beyond the traditional establishment, can we reach and embolden to be part of that debate?

Of all the changes Haass made to the classic work at the Council, the greatest transformation took place in the Studies Program. Haass understood that being a director of Studies was an all-consuming, hugely important task. In fact, Gelb had tried to steal Haass from Brookings in the 1990s to serve as the Council's director of Studies, but Haass had declined, saying, "Les, this will not be good for our friendship. You've gone through several Studies directors. I'd rather be your friend than your employee." He understood that Gelb had done the department few favors by having a multitude of directors come and go, so one of Haass's first hires was James M. Lindsay, a clear writer and no-nonsense thinker whom he knew from Brookings, where Lindsay was a senior fellow. Lindsay arrived at the Council the same year that *America Unbound: The Bush Revolution in Foreign Policy*, a book he coauthored with Ivo Daalder, received a number of awards and was selected as a top book of 2003 by the *Economist*. Lindsay would set a high bar for the Studies Program.

Together, Haass and Lindsay put Studies on a steady course. They agreed to mutually approve new fellows and sign off on ideas for book-length manuscripts. Fellows had to adhere to a "book-first,

Isobel Coleman and James M. Lindsay at the 2006 National Conference

but not book-only culture," in which they prioritized their work on a manuscript while taking time to distill their book projects into occasional articles and op-eds in leading papers and journals and take part in briefings with policymakers, journalists, and corporate members. The expectations grew over time, particularly as social networking became a bigger means of outreach, and fellows were expected to contribute to blogs, Twitter, podcasts, and interactive features on the Council's website. Lindsay has spent countless hours encouraging the fellows, debating their arguments, and commenting on their draft manuscripts, and Haass has reviewed every book manuscript alongside outside reviewers. The efforts have paid off, and over the years they have added fellows who were thought leaders and would shape the foreign policy debates through their work.

Between 2004 and 2020, more than one hundred books came out of the work of the Studies Program. In 2005, Studies made a mark with Elizabeth Economy's book *The River Runs Black* and Stephen Flynn's *America the Vulnerable*. The former laid bare the environmental devastation of China's rushed development; the latter painted

Participants at the 2016 Religion and Foreign Policy Workshop

a worrying picture of America's ability to deal with future terror attacks. Flynn would brief many government officials, and his work informed Bush's and Obama's policies on domestic security. Over the summer of 2007, fellows published fifty op-eds, and several new books were in press: Vali Nasr's *The Shia Revival*, Ray Takeyh's *Hidden Iran*, and Max Boot's *War Made New*. Nasr briefed President Bush on Iraq, while other fellows testified before Senate and House committees in Washington, DC.

The list of compelling books steadily grew. Edward Alden's *The Closing of the American Border: Terrorism, Immigration, and Security Since 9/11* (2008) demonstrated the economic and social consequences of policymakers' messing with border control for political gain; Benn Steil's *The Battle of Bretton Woods* (2013) and *The Marshall Plan: Dawn of the Cold War* (2018) were lavished with awards; Micah Zenko's *Red Team: How to Succeed by Thinking Like the Enemy* (2015) became a critical part of war college syllabi; Max Boot's *The Road Not Taken: Edward Lansdale and the American Tragedy in Vietnam* (2018) was a finalist for a Pulitzer Prize; and Thomas Bollyky's *Plagues and the Paradox of Progress: Why the World Is Getting Healthier in Worri-some Ways* (2018) pointed out serious gaps in global health well before the COVID-19 pandemic.

While Haass was updating the classic work that was at the heart of the Council, he was also steadily transforming the public face of the organization. As vice president of global communications and media relations, Lisa Shields was charged with making the Council's work more available to media and to broader audiences—work that began at the millennium when Les Gelb asked her to create a website ana-lyzing issues and debates ahead of the 2000 U.S. elections. The desire for the Council and *Foreign Affairs* to offer accessible expertise to the public greatly intensified after 9/11, when media and broader audi-ences were urgently and anxiously trying to make sense of a world that seemed so unfamiliar and precarious.

The 2005 redesign of CFR.org was an important aspect of the Council's work to inform the public. The website no longer carried only Council publications; it featured solid work from other think tanks and media outlets with an eye toward becoming a popular and reliable source of information on international affairs. It also gave the media and public more frequent and fresher views into the work of Council experts, especially when the work intersected with inter-national crises.

Shields explains,

> When I first got to the Council in 1999, few in the media thought of CFR as a go-to source for analysis of breaking global events. My phone rarely rang. But as we built up the website and held in-person press briefings with our experts, we got into the business of analyzing breaking news, and we quickly became good at it. For example, after the tragic assassination of Benazir Bhutto on December 27, 2007, we set up a call with our Pakistan expert Dan Markey, and hundreds of journalists around the world dialed in to hear his thoughts and analysis. From then on, we greatly expanded the frequency of the briefings as well as the content on the website that was aimed at presenting serious yet accessible analysis about the issues of our time.

The work paid off. In 2020, CFR and *Foreign Affairs*' websites received a collective twenty-six million unique visitors who were eager to consume what the organization had to offer.

A TURNING POINT

The Council's eighty-fifth anniversary was shaping up to be a great year. The relaunched Council website was bringing in a record number of visitors. A new Outreach initiative on the role of religion in U.S. foreign policy kicked off, and another program was added to include state and local officials and community leaders. Members voted to expand the Board from thirty-one to thirty-six members, resulting in a more diverse group that incorporated eleven women and six people of color, including Black, Asian, and Latinx members.

More important, the new capital campaign, designed to raise $85 million to sustainably resource the Council, was moving quickly toward its goal. The campaign eventually raised $123 million, a large portion coming from a small number of billionaire benefactors. This was a legacy of the old Council, where the financial leadership and impetus for giving came from three Board members: Peterson, Greenberg, and Rockefeller. They were prepared to step up and give generously. As Haass put it, "All three of them loved this institution."

At the same time, 2006 was a turning point. It was the last year that northeastern titans would represent such a large proportion of giving to the Council. Thanks to Suzanne E. Helm, whom Haass knew from the Brookings Institution and hired to lead development and philanthropic giving to the Council, the campaign served as a way to encourage more members to give irrespective of their wealth. Helm explained that the Council's pool of donors had been too small and that Haass

---

Following pages: Council members gather in New York for the Council's eighty-fifth anniversary gala in 2006.

realized early on that he needed to bring Council fund-raising into a more contemporary mode, where you are not reliant on a handful of donors that you approach from time to time, and that you are democratizing it and branching out. He understood that he needed member-ship to understand that this was not just a club. It was a nonprofit, and dues only paid part of the rent.

Dues that year made up 12 percent of the $35 million operating budget.

The development strategy was part of a new approach to running the Council, one that recognized that the best way to do good, impact-ful work on international affairs in the twenty-first century was with a professionalized organization, one that is staff-led, with the Board one step removed. The expansion of giving to the Council had several effects. It created a greater balance with the Board, empowered staff, and cushioned the blow of the 2008 financial crisis.

Haass noted, "We got through the financial crisis. We didn't have to lay one person off because of it. We stayed in the black. It was tough. We tightened our belts. We went a year or two without any salary increases. We reduced our bonus pool dramatically for a year. We didn't fill certain slots when they became open. But we kept doing pretty much everything we needed to do." David Bradley, chair of Atlantic Media, acknowledged the Council's strengths when he stepped down in 2019 after ten years on its Board: "I just want to say that I've been involved in a lot of nonprofits. This is the best-run nonprofit I've been involved in."

The strategy to resource the Council in new ways also opened the door to a much greater role for the organization in Washington, DC, with plans for a dedicated building. Since 1972, the Council had rented many spaces in the nation's capital, including at the Carnegie Endowment for International Peace. This limited the capacity of meet-ings and programs for local members and policymakers in Congress, the State Department, and other government institutions. It created the impression that the Council did not take Washington seriously, and some directors were eager to correct this view. Other Board mem-bers were not supportive; they worried about cost and fretted that a larger operation in Washington would bifurcate the Council. Haass said, "There were people who were worried I was going to bring a big truck up to East 68th Street and somehow cart the Council to Wash-ington in the dead of night and recenter it there."

Carla Hills, the Council's first female co-chair from 2007 to 2017, backed Haass and steered the Council on where to buy property. They

Council Co-chairs Robert E. Rubin and Carla A. Hills at the unveiling ceremony for their official portraits, 2017

passed up several locations, including a stately property on Dupont Circle that President Coolidge had occupied while the White House was being renovated in the 1920s. They chose a plainer building; its biggest selling points were that the footprint of the property allowed for a modern wing to be added and that it was a short walk from the White House, the U.S. trade representative's office, and the State Department. Thanks to the work of the Council's Vice President Nancy E. Roman and other staff and members of the Board, the building at 1777 F Street, NW opened on budget and on time in January 2009, five years after the number of Washington members had caught up with New York's.

The Council still retained its nucleus of traditional activities. Task forces and meetings continued as before—some humdrum, others edifying, and a few concluding in dissent. Madeleine Albright co-chaired the Independent Task Force that produced the report

Following pages: The Council's office in Washington, DC

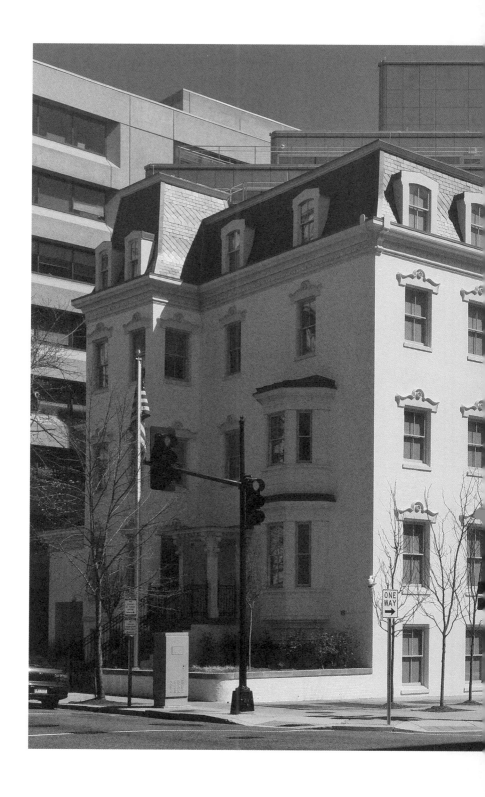

Brent Scowcroft (center), Samuel R. Berger (right), and William Nash at the 2005 release of the Task Force report on U.S. postconflict capabilities

In Support of Arab Democracy, and Brent Scowcroft co-chaired the Independent Task Force that produced *In the Wake of War: Improving U.S. Post-Conflict Capabilities*, which the policy community received as much-needed, quality, nonpartisan work despite the wide rift between Republicans and Democrats on many international and domestic issues. Carla Hills and retired Admiral Dennis C. Blair co-chaired an Independent Task Force that produced *U.S.-China Relations: An Affirmative Agenda, A Responsible Course*. The report laid out the political and economic concerns of both sides and identified areas of mutually beneficial cooperation.

At events of the Meetings Program, members continued to see world leaders up close, as they had in the earliest days of the Council. With some events now on the record, politicians were far more guarded and scripted. But sparks flew occasionally. The Council invited Iranian President Mahmoud Ahmadinejad to speak in 2006, at a time when the Bush administration was increasing pressure on Tehran's nuclear program. The invitation divided the Board and membership because Ahmadinejad had made public comments doubting the Holocaust. A decision was made to press ahead with a smaller meeting off-site, in part to accommodate the demands of the Iranian

Iranian President Mahmoud Ahmadinejad speaks with Council members in 2006.

delegation. Greenberg, who served in World War II and was one of the first to see the Dachau concentration camp after it had been liberated, told Ahmadinejad, "You don't know what you are talking about. I happened to be there." A flustered Ahmadinejad demanded to know Greenberg's age, claiming he did not look old enough to have fought in the war.

Sometimes the meetings were important just to get a sense of a leader's demeanor and size them up. One Board member explained, "I went to hear Nouri al-Maliki, who came from Iraq . . . and he came across as a weak, spineless kind of guy—his persona, his body language, his being showed you what he was." Fareed Zakaria, who returned to the Council as a Board member during Haass's tenure, affirmed this sentiment as he looked back on events he attended over the years:

> UN week is always crazy because there is this caval-
> cade of heads of state that come in. One day we had
> Pervez Musharraf and Hugo Chávez both on the same
> day. Musharraf comes in and is this completely typical
> general—very, very straight, very precise, very by the

book, and very dull. Then Chávez comes in, and he charms the crowd. I remember vividly because I was sitting next to him at his table for lunch. He was just so garrulous and funny, and he was quoting [Walt] Whitman and baseball and talking about how much he loved America. . . . Here you had this rogue but a charming rogue. . . . It made you understand why Chávez is popular—the power of that kind of populism is often wrapped up with a charismatic personality.

WIDENING THE MEMBERSHIP

Global stock markets plunged in 2008, and food riots erupted in low-income countries. Kosovo became independent with the support of the United States, while Russia and Georgia went to war over the breakaway regions of Abkhazia and South Ossetia. In Asia, hundreds of thousands died when a cyclone smashed into Myanmar, and an earthquake devastated China's Sichuan Province. A new gadget called the iPhone was proliferating, Spotify was launched, and New Yorkers were humming Alicia Keys's songs. Words such as *photobomb* and *mansplain* had entered the English language. The November 5 *New York Times* headline read, "OBAMA: Racial Barrier Falls in Decisive Victory."

That same year, a billionaire philanthropist, a former secretary of state, and a blockbuster actor headlined at the Council. Melinda Gates made a case for a different brand of philanthropy, one in which governments, foundations, and the private sector work together to solve the greatest challenges in global health and poverty. The Gates Foundation had shown the way, working with the Bush administration, industrialized donor countries, the World Health Organization, and pharmaceutical companies to get lifesaving vaccines to 175 million children in the poorest countries and affordable antiretroviral drugs to fight the HIV epidemic in Africa.

Condoleezza Rice gave a keynote that June at the fortieth anniversary of the International Affairs Fellowship and thanked the program for giving her the chance as a young academic to enter government service. In 1985, the fellowship had placed the then assistant professor of international relations at Stanford University with the Joint Chiefs of Staff to work on arms control policies. The fellowship, she told all assembled, "was indeed one of the best, best experiences" of her life.

Angelina Jolie at the Council, 2008

Chatting with Council Board member Richard E. Salomon on stage in front of 160 former, current, and future fellows and Council members, she reflected on the lessons of the past eight years with the Bush administration and laid out her vision for the future of U.S. foreign policy. There was some grumbling in the hallways, as Rice was identified with the unpopular Iraq War, but when she spoke everyone listened, she commanded respect, and a feeling of exhilaration spread among the new international affairs fellows of what the experience would hold in store for them.

Angelina Jolie's visit sparked surprising divisions, with more than one member raising concerns: embracing Hollywood stars would cheapen the CFR brand, lower the standards, and open the doors to members who had nothing of substance to say. But Jolie was no lightweight. She had made her mark working on refugee issues with the International Red Cross, and she knew the data, the debates, and what was at stake in ending civil conflicts justly, even as she delivered her remarks in a self-effacing way:

> I don't know if the International Criminal Court is the answer, and I don't know what type of court is or what it would need to be for all of us to agree and make it strong enough. I have no idea. And after seven years of traveling to the field, I find that I have a lot that I need to learn. But I do know this: No mother who had her children killed in

---

Facing page top: *Melinda Gates with Tom Brokaw*

Facing page bottom: *Condoleezza Rice and Richard E. Salomon*

Heidi Crebo-Rediker, Thomas R. Nides, and Lareina Yee at a Women and Foreign Policy event, 2017

front of her, no young girl sold into slavery, no boy kid-napped and forced to be a child soldier, and no young girl like the three-year-old I met in Sierra Leone who had her limbs cut off should be simply expected to forget. No one should be forced to choose between peace and justice.

One senior staff member said, "Anyone who actually saw her would come away thinking she was smart, she was serious, and she was informed. She clearly did not want to be a distraction or draw undue attention to herself, but she knew that she had the potential to generate huge amounts of attention and thus could raise awareness as a way to make the most impact." Members jostled to meet with her, but, if they were hoping for a bit of Hollywood glitter, they would have been disappointed. *Foreign Affairs* Editor Gideon Rose laughed about what people imagined as opposed to what she delivered, saying, "She was really, really serious about refugees, and she embodied what it meant to be an appropriate member of the Council."

As Nancy D. Bodurtha, vice president of Meetings and Member-ship at the Council, explained, "Jolie was not the first movie star to join the Council. Hollywood child star–turned-diplomat Shirley

Temple Black became a member in 1977." But this was an exception, and it was only later in the 1990s that Gelb opened the Council to others from Hollywood including Richard Dreyfuss, Warren Beatty, and Michael Douglas. Bodurtha remembers that actor Ron Silver, known for *The West Wing* and *Enemies, A Love Story*, also became a member during Gelb's tenure. "Silver's election to membership was controversial among some members for the same reasons as Jolie's, even though he spoke Mandarin and had a master's degree in Chinese history," she said.

Gelb started a trend that Richard Haass was able to take to the next level. In expanding membership and the range of voices speaking there, the Council was going well beyond the northeastern elite to embrace other sectors, including Hollywood. Jolie's presence was part of a new direction at the Council, valuing people for their contributions to global affairs no matter their industry.

That the three notable speakers in 2008 were women was also a sign that the Council could rise to the challenges of gender equity. Among the Council's programs was one on Women and Foreign Policy, which Gelb started thirty years after the first women joined the Council as members. And a 2018 meeting in New York, "Closing the Gap: Achieving Gender Parity in the C-Suite," featured leaders such as Ellen J. Kullman, the former CEO of DuPont, speaking on what needed to be done to promote equality in the workplace.

FOREIGN AFFAIRS IN THE DIGITAL AGE

Not since Hamilton Armstrong replaced Archibald Cary Coolidge in 1928 had a managing editor risen to the top of the masthead at *Foreign Affairs.* The norm at the magazine was to recruit a chief from the outside. But in October 2010, when James F. Hoge Jr. decided to retire, Gideon Rose, the managing editor working under Hoge, was a top contender and had unanimous support from the search committee.

As a managing editor in the early 2000s, Rose was a creative workhorse, eager to expand the magazine beyond its paper format. *Foreign Affairs* had been late to the online game. It had a website that was a mirror of the print edition and not much more. With the support of David Kellogg, the Council's publisher, Rose got Hoge to agree to experiment with digital content. *Foreign Affairs* was a small shop, and the staff had to find a way to make the internet work for them rather than follow where the internet would take them. For half a decade, magazine blogs were proliferating with content that was ephemeral, substantively uneven, and unappealing for a magazine focused on quality.

Rose pioneered short, online-only pieces, such as "Snapshots," articles with fewer than one thousand words yet worthy of archiving and of the *Foreign Affairs* imprimatur. The pieces had to conform to a four-part catechism: important, authoritative, accessibly argued, and attractively presented. But few authors naturally wrote with those principles in mind. Rose laughed as he summed it up, "We get our

---

Facing page top: Fareed Zakaria, James F. Hoge Jr., and Gideon Rose

Facing page bottom: The magazine's website, 2001

FOREIGN AFFAIRS

Global Survey
The best thinking from the past and present

REGIONAL:
Africa
The Americas
Asia
Australasia and the Pacific
Europe
Middle East
Russia, CIS, and Central Asia
South Asia

TOPICS:
Arms Control, Nuclear Weapons and Disarmament
Culture and Religion
Defense and Military Issues
Economics, Trade and Finance
Energy and Natural Resources
Environment
Globalization
Human Rights
Intelligence
International Law
International Organizations
Media/Public Opinion
Peacekeeping/ Preventive Action
Political Systems
Population and Demography
Presidency
Science and Technology
Terrorism
Theory
U.S. Policy and Politics

Background Briefings

A World of Change

Testing the Global Economy »
U.S. role in globalization, the impact of Doha, needed economic collaboration   *Updated 12/3/01*

Targeting Saddam? »
Containing Iraq while approaching Iran, Libyan rehabilitation, and the fallout from the war on terrorism   *Updated 12/3/01*

The Oil Market: A Barrel of Uncertainty »
Price wars, U.S. energy strategies, oil and instability in the Middle East   *Updated 12/3/01*

New Book on Terrorism from *Foreign Affairs*

In the aftermath of the terrorist attacks on September 11, one question has been on everyone's mind: "How did this happen?" The editors of *Foreign Affairs* have brought together noted experts whose insights make the events of that terrible day more understandable, even as we steel ourselves for the conflicts ahead. More information »

In the November / December 2001 Issue

Blowback in the Middle East
The drumbeat of anti-Americanism in the Middle East grew steadily after the Gulf War, finally erupting on September 11. Fouad Ajami of Johns Hopkins University's School of Advanced International Studies asks which governments can the United States really count on, and at what price? *The Sentry's Solitude* - click for full text

The Argentine Experiment Unravels
Argentina's economic meltdown has sparked fears of contagion elsewhere in Latin America. Manuel Pastor of the University of California, Santa Cruz, and Carol Wise of Johns Hopkins' School of Advanced International Studies look at why Argentina has become a Latin American nightmare-and ask what will happen next. *From Poster Child to Basket Case* - click for full text

Leading the Free World
Even after September 11, David Halberstam's analysis of Washington's

FOREIGN AFFAIRS

Published by the Council on Foreign Relations ©2001

ATTENTION:::

Researchers & Educators

CONNECT with Foreign Affairs Partners and Advertisers

Carnegie Council on Ethics & International Affairs

The Center for Policy Analysis on Palestine

articles from the horse's mouth, but the problem is that they are often written in horse."

Once he took over *Foreign Affairs*, Rose and his team continued to expand the website, putting great thought into how to reach new audiences and expand both web traffic and subscriptions without departing from the "eternal form" that had made *Foreign Affairs* great. A more substantial change soon followed, when Rose and Mia Higgins, the Council's first general counsel, reorganized the magazine to bring the editorial and business sides together. Subscriptions hit a new record, passing two hundred thousand for the first time in 2016, and online traffic increased substantially. In 2017, Rose hired Daniel Kurtz-Phelan as his executive editor. Kurtz-Phelan had previously worked as the magazine's senior editor before going on to serve on the policy planning staff of the State Department during the Obama administration. His return to *Foreign Affairs* was continuing the decades-long tradition of strong managing editors, and he became the chief editor of the magazine when Rose stepped down in January 2021.

Foreign Affairs had become exceptionally strong and successful by virtue of Rose's decade of leadership. In a single day in May 2020, in the midst of the COVID-19 pandemic, the website saw 313,507 visits, 73 percent over the previous record, an indicator that *Foreign Affairs* was meeting the public's desire for solid, reliable analysis and argument during times of crisis. That same week, Rose was gratified to learn that George Soros, the billionaire financier-philanthropist and bête noire of the populist right, was looking forward to talking with Steven Mnuchin, President Donald J. Trump's secretary of the treasury, about a *Foreign Affairs* article, "Chinese Debt Could Cause Emerging Markets to Implode" by Benn Steil and Benjamin Della Rocca.

While Rose is a powerful writer in his own right, nothing pleased him more than seeing people he published do well:

> A true editor's soul has to be informed by the Yiddish concept of *shepping naches*, usually defined as taking vicarious pleasure in somebody else's accomplishment. Like what a parent feels when their child stars in the school play. A true editor *sheps naches* when their author becomes a star. Gore Vidal once quipped that every time one of his friends succeeded, he dies a little. It's such a horrible line, and it represents the exact opposite of what a good editor should feel, because you can't compete with your authors. You should bask in their reflected glory.

AN ADDITIONAL MISSION: EDUCATION

By 2012, Haass had improved the Council, diversified its membership, and expanded its bread-and-butter work. CFR.org had expanded its coverage with new features, such as Policy Innovation Memoranda and blogs, bringing more traffic to the website (a 30 percent increase in late 2011 and early 2012). "Ask CFR Experts" and livestreamed meetings were now part of public outreach, adding to the number of people visiting CFR.org.

The Council of Councils, a consortium of leading think tanks mostly from Group of Twenty countries, was formed in March 2012 to discuss the state of global governance and multilateral cooperation. It drew on the best thinking around the world to find common ground on shared threats, build support for innovative ideas, and introduce remedies into the public debate and policymaking processes of member countries. Its annual Report Card on International Cooperation evaluated global efforts on ten issues and cited climate change as the top global priority in 2019. The report card gave global cooperation an overall C grade, a sign that talk of an "international community" remains aspirational in many ways.

Several months after the Council of Councils was formed, CFR inaugurated its Global Board of Advisors, led by David Rubenstein. The Board included people such as former Secretary-General of the United Nations Kofi Annan and Saudi business executive Lubna Olayan, who would later become the first woman to head a Saudi bank.

Studies had grown to 134 staff, thanks to successful fundraising efforts and good financial management. The Council won the 2012 UnitedHealthcare Well Deserved Award, and the American Heart Association would designate the Council a 2013 Fit Friendly

Worksite (Gold Level) in recognition of its innovative health and wellness programs.

The Council's diversity had notably increased as well. Women made up 56 percent and minority groups 28 percent of staff. Of the Council's 4,500 members in 2012, 26 percent were women, and 15 percent belonged to minority groups. The numbers were more encouraging in the Term Member Program; women made up 40 percent and minorities 25 percent of this younger cohort.

Hills and Rubin encouraged many of the changes by virtue of their role as co-chairs, exercising the role of the Board in steering the Council while letting Haass lead as an empowered president. They knew when to step back and when to step in, and Haass had their full support. In turn, Haass was able to create new teams to manage and professionalize the organization—adding an in-house counsel, an investment team, and a chief financial officer. The Council was on a secure and confident footing. But was there enough reason for him to stay?

An answer came during a fishing trip in Nantucket that summer with a friend. The friend had brought along his nephew, a Stanford student majoring in computer science and about to start his senior year. Haass was surprised to learn that the student had had almost no classes in history, economics, and international relations. "What was clear was that this intelligent young man would soon graduate from one of the best universities with little or no understanding of his country or the world," Haass recounted. Haass decided that there was a lot more work to do at the Council.

In 2014, the Council inaugurated its Education Program, with a mission that departed from the Council's classic focus and way of working. Since 1936, the Council had worked with academia to organize occasional conferences, and it included among its members and study groups professors and graduate students who were experts in international affairs. Renewing America, a Council-wide initiative, had examined how the state of K–12 education, infrastructure, debt, and immigration was affecting America's standing in the world. This included a Task Force on U.S. education reform and national security, co-chaired by Condoleezza Rice and former Chancellor of the New York City Department of Education Joel I. Klein. The Task Force argued that the failure to educate students was impairing the country's ability to thrive in a global economy, threatening long-term national security, and set forth a series of recommendations to reverse the decline in education.

Dutch students participating in a Model Diplomacy session on a visit to CFR, 2019

But the mission of the Education Program was radically new for the Council. Although Studies work and meetings on education were not new, the Council had never developed educational, curricular material. The Education Program would change this and work with Outreach to encourage institutions of higher learning in the United States to integrate international relations and world politics into their curricula for all students, no matter their intended major.

Through the leadership of Vice President of Education Caroline Netchvolodoff, the Council soon rolled out two major products: Model Diplomacy, which featured simulations of National Security Council meetings for students to role-play and learn how to write policy memos in response to international crises, and World101, an online library of free modules on the fundamentals of international relations, which the American Association of School Librarians named one of the best digital tools in 2020.

The Council made the material freely available to high schools and state and community colleges, whose resources are more constrained than those of the Ivy League and wealthier liberal arts colleges. Haass's book *The World: A Brief Introduction* (2020) was the newest tool at students' disposal, offering those who normally would not be exposed to international relations a digestible way to become informed about foreign policy, arrive at independent judgments, and hold politicians to account for the policy choices they make.

Disseminating the work was tough but rewarding for the staff of the Education Program, aided by people in Outreach who helped get the message out. Vice President of the National Program and Outreach Irina A. Faskianos leads the Council's efforts to reach constituencies whose work intersects with foreign policy issues but who find themselves outside of the typical foreign policymaking circles. These audiences include state and local officials, local journalists, religious leaders, and academics and educators. But reaching educators can be challenging, particularly for the small outreach team Faskianos leads. She explained, "We are not Penguin. We don't have a huge sales force that hits colleges and professors." Haass pitched in as much as possible, giving virtual book talks in 2020 that reached hundreds of schools. Suzanne Helm added, "The launch of the Education work really jazzed people to give to the Council. Many members and people on the Board were incredibly generous in funding work to bring international relations to the average American."

THE COUNCIL IN THE AGE OF TRUMP

❝ Everyone who works at CFR must be willing to brief any candidate." Having briefed Donald Trump, the Republican contender for the nomination, in October 2015, Haass reminded Council fellows that, irrespective of their own political affiliation, they were bound by the Council's principles of nonpartisanship to inform all political elites, including disruptors who did not play by the rules. Naturally, the duty to inform did not mean supporting their policies, and Trump became the subject of a torrent of critical articles by Council directors, members, and fellows after winning the presidency and formulating his first policies under the America First mantra.

In 2017, Haass argued in *Foreign Affairs* that the Trump presidency's penchant for improvisation was dangerous and advised what the president should and should not do in order to reboot American foreign policy. True to his belief in the lessons of history, Haass wrote:

> Back during the George W. Bush administration, in trying to articulate what the United States really wanted from China, Robert Zoellick, the deputy secretary of state, framed the question as one of whether Beijing was prepared to act as "a responsible stakeholder" in the international system. The concept is a useful one and applies now to the United States, the founder and dominant power within that system. So what constitutes responsible behavior for Washington in the world at large at this juncture?

Haass had been thinking about America's role and responsibility for a long time, even more so after coming to the Council in 2003. In those first years, the most salient debate was between realists and

Trump supporters at a rally in Des Moines, Iowa, 2020

neoconservatives. As he described in *War of Necessity, War of Choice: A Memoir of Two Iraq Wars*, a fundamental rift had formed between neoconservatives in the George W. Bush administration, who used the 2003 Iraq War as a fateful attempt to turn Iraq into a democracy, and realists, who pointed to the limited goals of the Gulf War in 1990–91, when George H.W. Bush managed to contain Iraq's adventurism without marching American troops into Baghdad. In his 2005 book, *The Opportunity: America's Moment to Alter History's Course*, Haass argued that the United States still had the chance to reshape the post–Cold War world without getting further drawn into a foreign policy that was all about transformation. At the time, the debates focused on what kind of foreign policy the United States should have.

But early in the Obama years, the debate about transformation receded. Haass explained,

> Obama, in many ways, consciously and unconsciously saw himself as not making the mistakes of his

CFR Chair David M. Rubenstein (right) interviews Jamie Dimon of JPMorgan Chase at the Council in 2019.

predecessor, George W. Bush. Instead he was going to be a more restrained president when it came to large-scale uses of military force, so he was going to avoid what he saw as the errors of Iraq and Afghanistan. And as is often the case in history and human existence, he overdid it.

Although American politics has periodically slipped into partisanship and dysfunctionality, Haass saw something qualitatively different about the rifts in the Obama years because of underlying trends in American society: polarization across all branches of government, gerrymandering, the rise of social media, and other factors that weakened the community and commonality of American politics. In

Following pages: The Council's leadership at the time of its centennial: Chair David M. Rubenstein, Vice Chairs Jami Miscik and Blair Effron, and President Richard N. Haass

167

169

Foreign Policy Begins at Home: The Case for Putting America's House in Order, Haass outlined the problems and warned that America would limit itself, underachieve at home, and have neither the resources nor mindset to be active in the world.

"Now under Trump, it's come full flower," Haass concluded. "But it's no longer the debate about what our priorities are in the world. It's more about whether the world should be a priority, and that, I think, is the big change. It began a bit under President Obama, but it has accelerated dramatically under President Trump, which is simply how much foreign policy we ought to have."

An additional challenge came about when it became apparent that the Trump administration did not value think tanks as sources of policy expertise. In January 2017, Josh Rogin wrote in the *Washington Post* that the Trump administration could cause the death of think tanks as we know them. Rather than relying on policy experts from think tanks, the Trump administration was drawing on business executives, former military leaders, and legions of private consultants who had direct lines of contact with and influence in the administration.

The same month, Tom Nichols, professor at the U.S. Naval War College, wrote an essay in *Foreign Affairs* about the loss of faith in expertise among the public and elected officials. "We are moving toward a Google-fueled, Wikipedia-based collapse of any division between professionals and laypeople," he wrote, and cited a recent poll in which primary voters were asked whether they would support bombing Agrabah. Nearly one-third of Republican respondents were in favor, just over one-third of Democratic voters were opposed, and the vast majority seemed unaware that Agrabah was a fictional kingdom in the 1992 Disney film *Aladdin*.

Yet, there was room to be upbeat about the future of the Council and its mission. The Studies Program that formed the intellectual heart of the Council had become stronger than in any period in its history. And although many other think tanks dotted the landscape—some highly specialized, others with a political bent—a strong sentiment at the Council persisted that Studies was unrivaled in quality, unmatched in its nonpartisan spirit, and guaranteed to play an outsized role in future policy debates. As Haass summed it up,

> Brookings' strength and weakness was that it covered everything and anything and that it was also perceived as liberal-leaning and that it talked to policy elites in Congress, the White House, and the State Department,

Richard N. Haass and PayPal CEO Daniel Schulman

with little effort to go beyond them. It was really trying
to influence the Washington debate. It's not wrong to
do that, but it limits your reach when DC becomes more
politicized and partisan.

In the twenty-first century, the Council had become far more than
a think tank and publisher. It had reasserted its role as an independent,
nonpartisan membership organization—one that does not take government money—and as a resource for all interested citizens to better
understand the world and the foreign policy choices facing the United
States and other countries. The Council's leadership, members, staff,
and directors recognized that foreign affairs touched everything, from
the American corporation that creates jobs and pays taxes to the state
governor who courts foreign investment to bring jobs to the state,
from a big city mayor who cannot adequately fight the pandemic without thinking about the rest of the world to a citizen who wants to make
an informed choice at the ballot box about a political candidate's foreign policy platform.

In that respect, the exchange between Haass and Daniel Schulman, president and CEO of PayPal, on the opening panel of the Council's 2017 Corporate Conference was meaningful to more than the few hundred members in the audience that day. Wearing a signature long-sleeved T-shirt and cowboy boots, Schulman spoke about PayPal's role in global monetary flows, its investments around the world, and how it has allowed hundreds of millions of people to bypass hard currency and use electronic funds transfers, providing a measure of financial independence to rich and poor, even in countries where politicians failed their people. PayPal was part of a major global transformation in a sphere of everyday life that governments and the banking sector had historically controlled. The event was just one of many examples of the Council in the twenty-first century broadening the conversation on foreign policy and global affairs in a way that transcended diplomats and policymakers.

A PANDEMIC POSTSCRIPT

On March 16, 2020, with the pandemic out of control in the Northeast, Council staff started working from home. All meetings and conferences shifted to virtual mode, a first in the Council's history. It was unsettling for an organization used to sociability, networking, and face-to-face discussions. By fortunate coincidence, Tom Frieden, the former head of the Centers for Disease Control and Prevention, had joined the staff as a senior fellow in early March 2020, and the Council had already launched a new website, ThinkGlobalHealth.org, aimed at the intersection of global health and other pressing global challenges. The website offered stark reminders of global inequities: women make up 70 percent of the global health workforce but only 25 percent of senior decision-making roles; more than 80 percent of people in South Asia and sub-Saharan Africa have no protections against illness or unemployment.

The Council had marked more than fifteen years of solid work in the sector since bringing Laurie Garrett on as its first global health fellow. Garrett made a splash with "The Next Pandemic?," an article she wrote for *Foreign Affairs* ten years before the Ebola outbreak in West Africa and fifteen years before the coronavirus pandemic. Garrett became one of the media's most sought-after experts when it came to pandemics and global health crises, and she became known as a fierce critic of lapses in global health institutions and insufficient preparedness in the United States.

The work of the Global Health program brought in other experts, including Yanzhong Huang, author of the 2020 book *Toxic Politics: China's Environmental Health Crisis and Its Challenge to the Chinese State*, and Thomas J. Bollyky, who launched the Think Global Health website and wrote on the growing challenge of noninfectious diseases such as cancer and diabetes in low-income countries. Adjunct Senior Fellow Catherine Powell coined the phrase "the color of COVID" in a CNN article that exposed the disproportionate effects of the pandemic on minority communities and women of color, who are the first to be sent to the front lines as essential workers, often without adequate protection.

During the pandemic, experts and the broader public flocked to the Council's website and *Foreign Affairs* for well-reasoned analysis. There they found much to read that was free of the destructive partisan debates and spin that increasingly divided the country.

Nearly one month before the pandemic shut down much of the Northeast, a February 18 Council meeting, "Threats to Global Health and Bio Security," forecasted that the pandemic would accelerate. Anthony S. Fauci, director of the National Institute of Allergy and Infectious Diseases, and Robert P. Kadlec, assistant secretary for preparedness and response at the U.S. Department of Health and Human Services, were the featured guests, speaking in the wake of China's lockdown of sixty million people in Wuhan Province, where the outbreak originated. Fauci warned that the United States did not appreciate the pandemic's looming magnitude and could face a mitigation scenario requiring "social distancing, keeping people at home, using teleworking, closing schools." Well before masks became a political statement and social distancing entered the everyday lexicon, the panel was a sign of things to come.

By April 7, when hospitals across the Northeast were overwhelmed and thousands of Americans had already died of COVID-19, Haass argued that the pandemic would hasten global trends, including the decline of U.S. power and the American model:

> Waning American leadership, faltering global cooperation, great-power discord: all of these characterized the international environment before the appearance of COVID-19, and the pandemic has brought them into sharper-than-ever relief. They are likely to be even more prominent features of the world that follows. . . . As a result, this crisis promises to be less of a turning point than a way station along the road that the world has been traveling for the past few decades.

Facing page top: *People around the world begin wearing masks in light of the pandemic.*

Facing page bottom: *CFR launched the Think Global Health website in 2020.*

Anthony S. Fauci, Robert P. Kadlec, and Frances Fragos Townsend speak at the Council in February 2020, three weeks before the Harold Pratt House would close due to the pandemic.

During the pandemic, Council events attracted record numbers of participants, governors and local officials dialed in to Council briefings to share best practices, and a shift in online learning increased interest in the Council's Education initiatives. Council members continued to find value in the organization even if they could not meet face-to-face at Pratt House or the Washington office. Henry Kissinger also went virtual on June 25, 2020, attracting over one thousand members to his Zoom talk on foreign policy and the lessons of history.

The Council offered its members, policymakers, and the interested public award-winning programs and publications. May 2020 saw a record-breaking 4.3 million visits to CFR.org and ForeignAffairs.com. Interactives such as the Global Conflict Tracker became the most-visited pages on CFR.org after the homepage. The Council had also greatly expanded its meetings and fellowship offerings. Newer types of meetings included the Lessons Learned series, Young Professionals Briefings, Master Classes, and the HBO What to Do About... series, which was run as a national security meeting in which speakers examined options to solve a foreign policy dilemma. The classic fellowship offerings of the Council expanded to include International Affairs Fellowships in Canada and India as well as for Tenured International Relations Scholars. The paid internship program, funded by the Blavatnik Family Foundation, gave over one hundred interns from many walks of life a first experience in the field of international affairs, including young people whose backgrounds are underrepresented in the field. Studies expanded with the support of Council Board member Bernard L. Schwartz to also study domestic issues at the core of America's well-being that determine prosperity at home and influence abroad. The Capital Campaign raised nearly $200 million from a diverse array of donors, new and old, securing the Council's work for posterity. The Council had become a program with many peers but few competitors.

In crisis, people searched for safe harbor, and many found it in the Council's work. The Council's stability and strength were reassuring in an unnerving time of global uncertainty, mounting deaths from the pandemic, and bitter political divisions in the United States, culminating in the riot at the U.S. Capitol and the historic inauguration of Joe Biden as the forty-sixth president and Kamala Harris as the first Black woman vice president.

• • •

On its one hundredth anniversary, the Council has much to celebrate. What began as a small membership organization created around a male, white elite of foreign policy practitioners, business titans, and academics has evolved into a twenty-first-century institution that is more than the sum of its parts. More than a membership organization, think tank, publisher, and public educator, the Council is, above all, an institution that represents American talent and nonpartisan ingenuity in addressing the toughest foreign policy dilemmas facing the United States and other countries.

The Council plays an ever-greater role as a talent developer, educating and training the policymakers and foreign affairs experts of the future. As Mira Rapp-Hooper testified, her modest beginning as a staff member on the Council's National Program was a turning point that gave her "a front-row seat to understand what careers in foreign policy look like." Council Vice President, Deputy Director of Studies, and Senior Fellow Shannon K. O'Neil shares her sentiment. O'Neil joined the Council in 2006 after exploring careers in investment banking and academia. As a fellow on Latin America, she wrote about trade issues. "We are much less integrated in North America than Europe and Asia," she explained, and it was important for her to understand the reasons and the opportunity costs of less trade. Early on as a fellow, she testified on the Hill about trade relations with Mexico alongside John Negroponte, the deputy secretary of state who went on to become the first director of national intelligence.

CFR Board member Tony Coles (second from right) and other Council members at the 2018 National Symposium in Menlo Park, California

"It was amazing, especially as it was at a time when I wasn't well known," O'Neil explained. "But the Council gave me the chance to talk to policymakers, and it got my name and work out in the public debates." When offered the position of deputy director of Studies, she accepted, seeing it as a chance to give new fellows the support and opportunities that she found elevating when she first started working at CFR.

In 2020, of the Council's 5,125 members, 39 percent reside outside the New York and Washington, DC, areas. Women make up 31 percent of membership and people of color 18 percent; these numbers will continue to rise as new members join (of those admitted to membership in February 2019, 46 percent were women and 34 percent people of color). The growing diversity at the Council is a work in progress, and more will be done—but what is clear is that the Council has changed to become more reflective of the American people.

In many ways, 2021 resembles the year the Council was founded. The specific issues that define international affairs are different, but overarching questions about how much of a role America should play in the world are the same. This makes the Council's nonpartisan work and mission as important as ever. As Alton Frye put it, "What impressed me in my first encounters with people in and around the Council was a clear understanding that, though some of them were long-term Democrats, some of them were long-term Republicans, they shared the sense that this institution was a precious element in American life precisely because it aspired to reach beyond partisan lines." And that's the short story of this past one hundred years.

ACKNOWLEDGMENTS

The short book in your hands is not the only history of the Council on Foreign Relations. Peter Grose's inside history, *Continuing the Inquiry: The Council on Foreign Relations From 1921 to 1996*, is sympathetic and atmospheric. Robert D. Schulzinger's *The Wise Men of Foreign Affairs: The History of the Council on Foreign Relations* is a good read from a critical, left-of-center viewpoint. Both provided wonderful material for this book, as did several anniversary monographs published by the Council in 1937, 1947, and 1960.

But this book is rather different. Much of the story is told as a living, breathing history through the stories of the people who experienced the Council as members, directors, fellows, and staff over the decades. There's nothing quite like hearing the story of an event or institution through the interviews of the Council on Foreign Relations Visual Oral History Project, conducted by the Columbia Center for Oral History. I use the interviews here, and I hope they convey intimacy and texture that we don't always get from archival documents. Nonetheless, to round out the sources, I consulted many primary-source documents at CFR's library and Princeton University's Seeley G. Mudd Manuscript Library. These are great resources for scholars, journalists, policymakers, and anyone interested in the Council's history as well as the broader subject of U.S. foreign policy.

If the story in these pages is enjoyable, it's thanks to the wonderful material I had available and to the many people who improved drafts along the way. My gratitude starts with all who participated in the oral history project, which was directed by Mary Marshall Clark at Columbia University. At CFR, Leigh Gusts, Alysse Jordan, and Connie Stagnaro were the most resourceful archivists and outstanding librarians. Connie spent many hours helping me track down vastly different bits of historical facts and data.

Nancy Bodurtha, Mona El-Ghobashy, Patricia Dorff, and Jim Lindsay gave many thoughtful comments, while Jessica Thomas, David Sacks, Sumit Poudyal, and Katherine De Chant provided editorial clarity.

Conversations with Irina Faskianos, Richard Haass, Suzanne Helm, Jim Lindsay, Shannon O'Neil, Mira Rapp-Hooper, and Lisa Shields filled in crucial pieces of the Council's more contemporary moments. Jim also kept me on my toes with his deep and nuanced knowledge of American history. Gideon Rose and Sarah Foster at *Foreign Affairs* helped me understand the magazine's story. For years, Gideon has shared riveting, edifying, funny, expletive-filled stories that always end with a moral or a lesson.

Jeff Reinke, true to his role as chief of staff at CFR, moved the book project along seamlessly and provided a keen sense of what mattered and how to balance priorities. Richard Haass read every draft and pushed me to see the bigger picture without missing the smaller details that add up when it comes to getting the history of a great institution right. He was very generous with his time and memorably started each meeting by asking me, "How can I help?"

ABOUT THE AUTHOR

George Gavrilis is a fellow at the Center for Democracy, Toleration, and Religion at the University of California, Berkeley, and works in the areas of international affairs and oral history. He also serves as a consultant to philanthropic institutions and international organizations, including the United Nations. Previously, he served as executive director of the Hollings Center for International Dialogue in Washington, DC, and Istanbul, Turkey. Gavrilis was a 2008–09 international affairs fellow with the Council on Foreign Relations placed with the UN Department of Political Affairs, Middle East and West Asia Division. Before then, he taught international relations and comparative politics at the University of Texas, Austin.

Gavrilis is the author of *The Dynamics of Interstate Boundaries*. His articles have appeared in *Foreign Affairs* and other journals. In the field of oral history, Gavrilis has served on projects for the Atlantic Philanthropies, the Carnegie Corporation of New York, the Council on Foreign Relations, the Harriman Institute, the Human Rights Campaign, and the Columbia Center for Oral History Research. He has a PhD in political science from Columbia University.

PHOTO CREDITS

p. 18, Frank B. Kellogg (Library of Congress)

p. 20, apple seller (Heritage Image Partnership Ltd/Alamy Stock Photo)

p. 21, Yosuke Matsuoka (courtesy of the *Oregonian*)

p. 21, Henry L. Stimson (Library of Congress)

p. 22, Nazi rally in Germany (National Archives)

p. 25, people reading about the German invasion of Poland (Library of Congress)

p. 26, Greenland in World War II (National Archives)

p. 27, Hamilton Fish Armstrong and Advisory Committee of Refugees (Alpha Stock/Alamy Stock Photo)

p. 28, Allied troops landing in Normandy (Library of Congress)

p. 34, George C. Marshall (Library of Congress)

p. 34, George F. Kennan (Library of Congress)

p. 35, atomic bomb test, 1949 (Library of Congress)

p. 38, Dwight D. Eisenhower (Everett Collection Historical/Alamy Stock Photo)

p. 40, the Akasaka Detached Palace (Keystone Press/Alamy Stock Photo)

pp. 46–47, command post of U.S. Air Force Strategic Air Command (National Archives)

p. 49, Chinese Communist Party rally (Alamy Stock Photo)

p. 52, Immanuel Klette (American Air Museum in Britain)

p. 52, Charles P. Tesh (NavSource Naval History)

p. 52, Malcolm Browne (AP Photo)

p. 52, Sidney Berry (The LIFE Picture Collection/Getty Images)

p. 57, anti-war protesters (Library of Congress)

p. 58, Hans Morgenthau (Jill Krementz, courtesy of Susanna Morgenthau)

p. 59, student occupation of Grayson Kirk's office (Larry Mulvehill, courtesy of *Columbia College Today*)

p. 60, U.S. soldiers in Vietnam (Library of Congress)

p. 66, Shirley Temple Black and Rita Hauser (UPI Telephoto)

p. 76, Ruth Bader Ginsburg (The Rockefeller Foundation)

p. 79, cars in line for gas (Alamy Stock Photo)

p. 83, Mobutu Sese Seko (Alamy Stock Photo)

p. 87, Singer and Pan Am logos (public domain)

p. 90, President Ronald Reagan (National Archives)

p. 97, Berlin Wall (INTERFOTO/Alamy Stock Photo)

p. 98, President George H.W. Bush addressing Congress (Mark Reinstein/Alamy Stock Photo)

p. 113, refugees fleeing from the former Yugoslavia (Dino Fracchia/Alamy Stock Photo)

p. 114, President Bill Clinton—NATO expansion (Robert Giroux/Reuters)

p. 123, Ralph Bunche (Los Angeles Public Library)